RAF, DOMINION & ALLIED SQUADRONS AT WAR:
STUDY, HISTORY AND STATISTICS

COMPILED BY
PHIL H. LISTEMANN

Drawings by Claveworks Classics

PREFACE

The purpose of this study is to provide aviation historians and enthusiasts with a range of information relative to each of the Commonwealth squadrons that saw combat during World War II. Each record will comprise a short history, complete with illustrations and artwork, and accompanied by the following appendices:

Appendix I: Squadron Commanders and Flight Commanders
Appendix II: Major awards
Appendix III: Operational diary (number of sorties per month)
Appendix IV: Victory list
Appendix V: Aircraft losses on operations
Appendix VI: Aircraft losses in accidents
Appendix VII: Aircraft Serial numbers matching with individual letters (including mission totals for multi-engine aircraft)
Appendix VIII: Nominal roll (Captains only for bomber and seaplane units)
Appendix IX: Roll of Honour

Individual files will be constantly updated, when any fresh information comes to light. Additional information will be available for download, at no charge, on each squadron's site at:

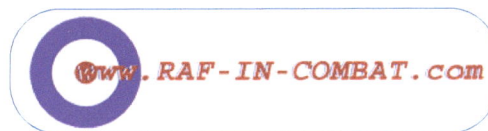

www.RAF-IN-COMBAT.com

GLOSSARY OF TERMS

RANKS

AC: Aircraftman
G/C: Group Captain
W/C: Wing Commander
S/L: Squadron Leader
F/L: Flight Lieutenant
F/O: Flying Officer
P/O: Pilot Officer
W/O: Warrant Officer
F/Sgt: Flight Sergeant
Sgt: Sergeant
Cpl: Corporal
LAC: Leading Aircraftman

OTHER

AAF: Auxiliary Air Force
CO: Commanding Officer
DFC: Distinguished Flying Cross

DFM: Distinguished Flying Medal
DSO: Distinguished Service Order
Eva.: Evaded
Inj.: Injured
ORB: Operational Record Book
OTU: Operational Training Unit
PAF: Polish Air Force
PoW: Prisoner of War
RAF: Royal Air Force
RAAF: Royal Australian Air Force
RCAF: Royal Canadian Air Force
RNZAF: Royal New Zealand Air Force
SAAF: South African Air Force
Sqn: Squadron
TOC: Taken on charge
†: Killed

No.131 Squadron (County of Kent) 1941-1945

ISBN: 978-2-918590-65-1

Contributors & Acknowledgments:
André Bar, Hugh Halliday, Drew Harrison, Pedley Family, Paul Sortehaug, Andrew Thomas,

Cover: Spitfire VII MD183 flying over the cloud.

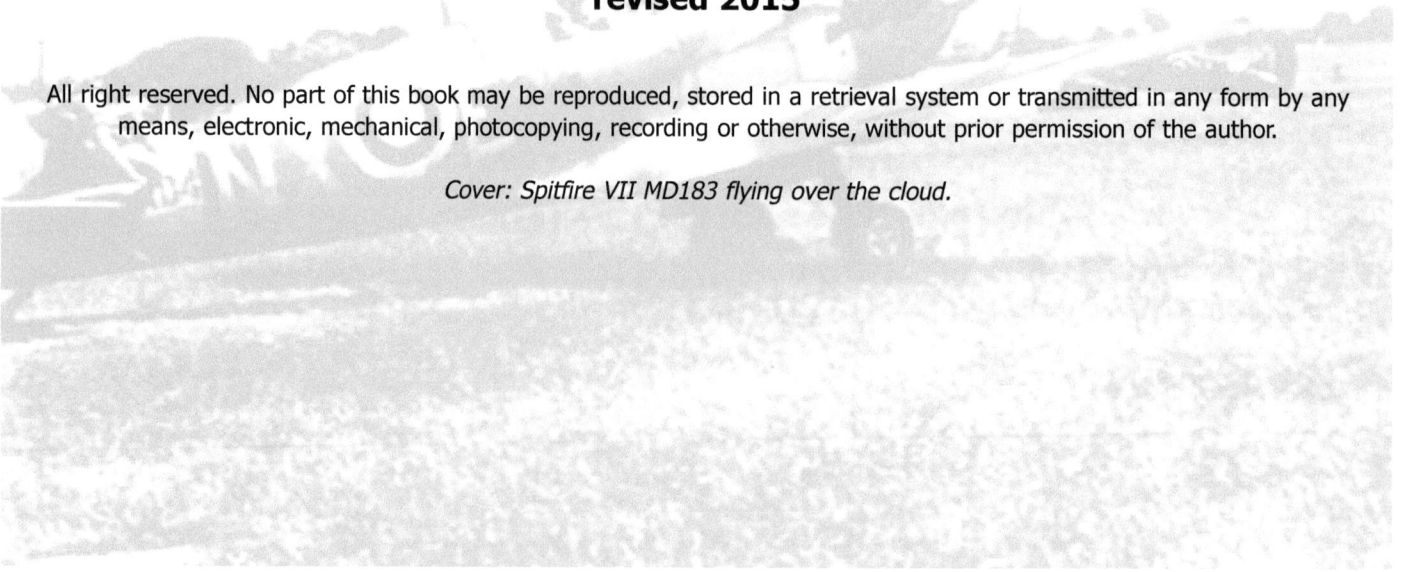

MAIN EQUIPMENT

SPITFIRE I	**Jun.41 - Nov.41**
SPITFIRE II	**Sep.41 - Jan.42**
SPITFIRE V	**Dec.41 - Sep.43**
SPITFIRE IX	**Sep.43 - Mar.44**
SPITFIRE VII	**Mar.44 - Oct.44**
SPITFIRE VIII	**Feb.45 - Jun.45**
THUNDERBOLT II	**Jun.45 - Dec.45**

SQUADRON CODE LETTERS:

NX

SQUADRON HISTORY

The Squadron was originally formed in 1918 but never became operational. In 1941 Fighter Command began to expand considerably and the 131 'number plate' was selected for a fighter squadron, with an official formation date of **30th June, 1941** at Ouston. The Squadron was placed under a veteran of the Battle of Britain, S/L J.M. Thompson, and worked up on the Spitfire, using Mk.Is first and then Mk.IIs. However, No.131 Sqn was unique from the beginning in having one of its flights - B Flight - formed with Belgian pilots, while the rest of the flying personnel who joined came from the Empire and beyond. Even though 131 Squadron became operational in October, activity was kept at a low level and can be seen as a false start. Indeed, the following month the Belgians left the Squadron to form a Belgian unit - No.350 (Belgian) Sqn - and had to be replaced, and training carried out with the new pilots. At the same time, S/L Thompson relinquished command to S/L M.G.F. Pedley the latter actually being the one who would lead the Squadron into action on a larger scale throughout 1942 flying the Spitfire Mk.V version, which at that time was the standard Spitfire model.

Success came in March when F/L R.H. Harries made the first claim of the Squadron when he shot down a Ju88 on the 12th, shared with a French pilot, Sgt A. Vilboux. The Squadron moved South in May, and sorties continued including participation in many fighter sweeps, *Rhubarbs* and other operations over the Continent, adding a couple of victories over German aircraft to its credit. The Squadron was involved in Operation 'Jubilee' on the 19th August 1942 over Dieppe, and claimed four confirmed victories that day. In January 1943, it flew North for some rest and spent six months on training and coastal patrols before going South again. In September 1943, 131 Squadron gave up its Spitfire Mk.Vs for Mk.IXs, the new standard version, but for a short time only as in March 1944, the Squadron was selected to receive the Mk.VII. The Spitfire Mk.VII was a high-altitude variant built in small numbers, making the Squadron one of the very few units to become operational on this type. From this point, the Squadron's main task became to provide high altitude escort for bombers but little opposition was met and only five claims were made – including four in August - before the Squadron moved to Friston. From that base, the Squadron was charged with providing escorts for Bomber Command's daylight raids, a task which was carried out until end of October when the Squadron ceased all operations to move to India as part of the reinforcement of the 3rd Tactical Air Force (3 TAF).

Squadron personnel arrived at Amarda Road in February 1945 but because of a lack of aircraft (131 Squadron now operated the Spitfire VIII) the number of hours flown for training remained low to a point where morale fell. In June the situation hadn't changed and the decision was taken to disband the unit on the 10th and to post away the personnel. The number plate was then given to No.134 Sqn, which was then flying Thunderbolts, a unit which was earmarked to participate to the liberation of Malaya. However the War with Japan ended before the Squadron became operational once more, and it eventually moved to Northern Malaya. Some dummy attacks were carried out in November to prevent riots, followed by leaflets raids but those remained the sole actions undertaken by the Squadron before it disbanded on **31st December, 1945**. If No.131 Squadron is not remembered by many as having been a Thunderbolt squadron, it must be remembered as having been one of the very few fighter squadrons to have flown six different marks of Spitfire even if its tally - 20 confirmed and probable claims - is not among the highest scores for Spitfire units.

SQUADRON BASES

Ouston	30.06.41 - 10.07.41	Merston	14.05.42 - 22.08.42
Catterick	10.07.41 - 06.08.41	Tangmere	22.08.42 - 24.08.42
Ternhill	06.08.41 - 27.09.41	Ipswich	24.08.42 - 31.08.42
Atcham	27.09.41 - 09.02.42	Tangmere	31.08.42 - 24.09.42
Llanbedr	09.02.42 - 04.03.42	Thorney Island	24.09.42 - 07.11.42
Valley	04.03.42 - 16.04.42	Westhampnett	07.11.42 - 22.01.43
Llanbedr	16.04.42 - 14.05.42	Castletown	22.01.43 - 26.06.43

Exeter	26.06.43 - 16.08.43	Friston		28.08.44 - ...
Redhill	16.08.43 - 17.09.43	*En route to FE*		
Church Stanton	17.09.43 - 10.02.44	Amarda Road (India)		05.02.45 - 03.04.45
Colerne	10.02.44 - 22.02.44	Dalbhumgarh (India)		03.04.45 - 10.06.45
Fairwood Common	22.02.44 - 29.02.44	Bobbili (India)		10.06.45 - 29.08.45
Colerne	29.02.44 - 24.03.44	Baigachi (India)		29.08.45 - 31.08.45
Harrowbeer	24.03.44 - 24.05.44	Zayatkwin (Burma)		31.08.45 - 11.09.45
Culmhead	24.05.44 - 28.08.44	Kuala Lumpur (Malaya)		11.09.45 - 31.12.45

APPENDIX I
SQUADRON AND FLIGHT COMMANDERS

Rank and Name	SN	Origin	Dates
S/L John M. **THOMPSON**	RAF No.34185	RAF	30.06.41 - 14.11.41
S/L Michael G.F. **PEDLEY**	RAF No.37328	RAF	14.11.41 - 31.08.42
S/L Peter R.W. **WICKHAM**	RAF No.33403	RAF	31.08.42 - 08.11.42
S/L John S. **FIFIELD**	RAF No.83274	RAF	08.11.42 - 20.03.43
S/L James J. **O'MEARA**	RAF No.40844	RAF	20.03.43 - 29.05.44
S/L Ian N. **MACDOUGALL**	RAF No.33491	RAF	29.05.44 - 14.10.44
S/L Constantine O.J. **PEGGE**	RAF No.41317	RAF	14.10.44 - 10.06.45
S/L Christopher G. **FORD**	RAF No.67659	RAF	10.06.45 - 22.09.45
F/L George M. **SMITH** (Temp.)	RAF No.134094	RAF	22.09.45 - 08.10.45
S/L John R. **GRAHAM** [1]	RAF No.116445	RAF	08.10.45 - 31.12.45

[1] Offically from 01.10.45, but he arrived at the Squadron on the 8th.

A Flight

F/L Frank E.W. **BIRCHFIELD**	RAF No.39777	RAF	05.07.41 - 14.01.42
F/L Raymond H. **HARRIES**	RAF No.87447	RAF	14.01.42 - 07.12.42
F/L Ralph W.L. **SAMPSON**	RAF No.116753	RAF	07.12.42 - 09.02.44
F/L Vincent K. **MOODY** (†)	Can./J.15362	RCAF	09.02.44 - 12.06.44
F/L John C.R. **WATERHOUSE**	RAF No.112749	RAF	19.06.44 - ??
F/L James E. **FRANKS**	Aus.403731	RAAF	10.06.45 - 31.07.45
F/L Norman G.S. **SALTER**	RAF No.149936	RAF	31.07.45 - ??.08.45
F/L George M. **SMITH**	RAF No.134094	RAF	??.08.45 - 31.12.45

B Flight

F/L Surry P.V. **BIRD**	RAF No.70064	RAF	02.07.41 - 25.09.41
F/L Henri A.C. **GONAY**	RAF No.81635	(BEL)/RAF	25.09.41 - 14.11.41
F/L John C.D. **DOLL**	RAF No.87445	RAF	17.11.41 - 13.01.43
F/L Tomas **KRUML**	RAF No.83229	(CZ)/RAF	13.01.43 - 23.02.43
F/L Tony G. **PICKERING**	RAF No.114471	RAF	23.02.43 - 06.01.44
F/L Clifford P. **RUDLAND**	RAF No.65998	RAF	06.01.44 - 06.08.44
F/L Cecil E. **BEARMAN** (†)	RAF No.122343	RAF	06.08.44 - 25.08.44
?			
F/L John P. **BLACKMORE**	RAF No.123096	RAF	10.06.45 - ??.08.45
F/L Ian A. **RATCLIFFE**	RAF No.163052	RAF	??.08.45 - 31.12.45

APPENDIX II
MAJOR AWARDS

DSO: 1
James Jospeh **O'MEARA** (No.40844 - RAF)

DFC: 4
Raymond Hiley **HARRIES** (No.87447 - RAF)
Michael George Forster **PEDLEY** (No.37328 - RAF)
Ralph William Frazer **SAMPSON** (No.116753 - RAF)
John Adam **SOWREY** (No.33551 - RAF)

DFM: -

APPENDIX III
OPERATIONAL DIARY
NUMBER OF SORTIES PER MONTH

Date	Month	Total	Date	Month	Total
			Jul.43	130	4,049
			Aug.43	248	4,297
			Sep.43	206	4,503
Sep.41	10	10	Oct.43	121	4,624
Oct.41	25	35	Nov.43	128	4,752
Nov.41	28	63	Dec.43	111	4,863
Dec.41	33	96	Jan.44	147	5,010
Jan.42	6	102	-	-	5,010
Feb.42	101	203	Mar.44	90	5,100
Apr.42	161	364	Apr.44	197	5,297
Mar.42	166	530	May.44	393	5,690
May.42	244	774	Jun.44	474	6,164
Jun.42	416	1,190	Jul.44	239	6,403
Jul.42	396	1,586	Aug.44	220	6,623
Aug.42	411	1,997	Sep.44	218	6,841
Sep.42	247	2,244	Oct.44	111	6,952
Oct.42	476	2,720	Oct-Nov 45	37	6,989
Nov.42	284	3,004			
Dec.42	212	3,216	**Grand Total**		**6,989**
Jan.43	75	3,291			
Feb.43	144	3,435			
Mar.43	149	3,584	Extracted from AIR27/940-941-942		
Apr.43	91	3,675			
May.43	134	3,809			
Jun.43	110	3,919			

APPENDIX IV
VICTORY LIST
CONFIRMED (C) AND PROBABLE (P) CLAIMS

Date	Pilot	SN	Origin	Type	Serial	Code	Nb	Cat.
		SPITFIRE V						
12.03.42	F/L Raymond H. HARRIES	RAF No.87447	RAF	Ju88	BL600	NX-H	0.5	C
	Sgt André P.F. VILBOUX	F.30330	FFAF		BL233		0.5	C
05.06.42	S/L Michael G.F. PEDLEY	RAF No.37328	RAF	Fw190	BM420	NX-A	1.0	P
	F/L Raymond H. HARRIES	RAF No.87447	RAF	Fw190	BL600	NX-H	1.0	P
	P/O Keith A.H. MASON	RAF No.111704	RAF	Fw190	EN764		1.0	P
09.06.42	P/O Keith A.H. MASON	RAF No.111704	RAF	Bf109	EN764		1.0	C
19.08.42	F/L Raymond H. HARRIES	RAF No.87447	RAF	Fw190	BL600	NX-H	1.0	C
				Do217	BL600	NX-H	0.25	C
	F/O Neil S. WILSON	RAF No.67105	RAF		AB364	NX-D	0.25	C
	P/O Albert F. ECKERT	CAN./J.15344	(US)/RCAF		EN773		0.25	C
	Sgt Alan W. BOWER	RAF No.778642	(SA)/RAF		EN791	NX-Z	0.25	C
	W/C Michael G.F. PEDLEY	RAF No.37328	RAF	Do217	BM420	NX-A	0.25	C
	Sgt Horace G. COPLAND	NZ41469	RNZAF		AD348	NX-C	0.25	C
	Sgt John D. THOROGOOD	RAF No.1293333	RAF		BL446		0.25	C
	Sgt John L. DAVIDSON	CAN./R.85602	RCAF		AB972	NX-R	0.25	C
	W/C Michael G.F. PEDLEY	RAF No.37328	RAF	Ju88	BM420	NX-A	0.33	C
	F/O Hugh S. JACKSON	RAF No.63098	RAF		EN830	NX-G	0.33	C
	Sgt Horace G. COPLAND	NZ41469	RNZAF		AD348	NX-C	0.33	C
	F/L John C.S. DOLL	RAF No.87445	RAF	Do217	EN893	NX-Q	0.25	P
	F/O Hugh S. JACKSON	RAF No.63098	RAF		EN830	NX-G	0.25	P
	P/O Emrys A.J. WILLIAMS	RAF No.117304	RAF		AA719	NX-S	0.25	P
	P/O Ivan K. CRAWFORD	RAF No.115189	RAF		AR378	NX-W	0.25	P
03.09.42	P/O Albert F. ECKERT	CAN./J.15344	(US)/RCAF	Fw190	BM429		1.0	C
06.12.42	F/L Raymond H. HARRIES	RAF No.87447	RAF	Fw190	EN944	NX-L	1.0	C
	P/O Henri L.L.F. DE BORDAS	F.30226	FFAF	Fw190	BL769	NX-Q	1.0	C
31.07.43	F/L Ralph W.L. SAMPSON	RAF No.116753	RAF	Fw190	BM121	NX-X	1.0	C
03.08.43	F/Sgt Robert K. PARRY	RAF No.1379966	RAF	Fw190	AB282	NX-G	1.0	P
		SPITFIRE VII						
12.06.44	F/O Robert K. PARRY	RAF No.156705	RAF	Bf109	MD187	NX-V	1.0	C
06.08.44	F/O Robert K. PARRY	RAF No.156705	RAF	Fw190	MD134	NX-P	1.0	C
	W/O Harold A. PATTON	AUS.414262	RAAF	Fw190	MD173		1.0	C
07.08.44	W/C Peter M. BROTHERS	RAF No.37668	RAF	Fw190	MD188	PB	1.0	C
	F/L Ralph W.L. SAMPSON	RAF No.116753	RAF	Fw190	MD165	NX-M	1.0	C
	F/L John C.R. WATERHOUSE	RAF No.112749	RAF	Fw190	MD152		1.0	C

Total: 21.0

Aircraft damaged : 17.0

APPENDIX V
AIRCRAFT LOST ON OPERATIONS

Date	Pilot		S/N	Origin	Serial	Code	Mark	Fate

SPITFIRE

27.03.42	Sgt Edward M. **OLDHAM**		AUS.402749	RAAF	**BL249**		VB	†

Took off on scramble at 14.05 with Sgt E.L. Mahar (RAAF) to intercept hostile raider. Missing off Isle of Wight, cause unknown. Searches were organised the following days but proved fruitless. Oldham, an Australian from New South Wales, had served with the squadron since November.
Note on the aircraft: TOC No.37 MU 23.11.41, issued to No.131 Sqn 10.12.41.

05.06.42	P/O Nathaniel W. **ROWELL**		RAF No.111130	RAF	**BL250**	NX-S	VB	†

Led by the CO the Squadron (12 aircraft) Took off at 14.50 for Circus 188 to Le Havre (France) with Nos.129 and 340 (Free French) Sqns, No.131 Sqn acting as top cover. On the return journey, 15 Enemy aircraft were seen flying above the formation which promptly attacked. Rowell broke formation to attack E/A and was never seen again. In return the squadron claimed three Fw190s probably destroyed (S/L Pedley and F/L Harries and P/O Mason) another damaged (P/O Mason). 'Bill' Rowell was a founder member of the squadron.
Note on the aircraft: TOC No.12 MU 01.12.41, issued to No.131 Sqn 12.12.41.

15.08.42	Sgt John **LUXFORD**		RAF No.657235	RAF	**AD554**		VB	†

Took off with Sgt Alan Bower (South African) at 09.00 to patrol St.Catherine's Point, Isle of Wight. Intercepted two Bf109s and in the ensuing combat Sgt Luxford called up to say that he would have to bale out, presuming that he was hit by Bf109s. He climbed and gave a fix which was acknowledged but Sgt Bower did not see any parachute. Sgt Luxford was never found. Luxford had joined the squadron in June.
Note on the aircraft: TOC No.24 MU 19.11.41, issued to No.131 Sqn 10.12.41.

22.10.42	F/O Neil S. **WILSON**		RAF No.67105	RAF	**EN791**	NX-Z	VB	†

Took off with eleven other at 11.55 for a fighter Roadstead to the Seine Estuary, F/L Ray Harries leading. At sea level to Le Havre, two armed trawlers were spotted and the squadron attacked. Hit by flak North of Ouistream (France), possibly in the radiator, and was forced to bale out. Pilot seen in his dinghy but was not rescued because of bad weather. 'Tug' Wilson had served with the squadron since July 1941.
Note on the aircraft: TOC No.45 MU 02.05.42, issued to No.131 Sqn 06.06.42.

24.10.42	F/Sgt John L. **DAVIDSON**		CAN./R.85602	RCAF	**AB850**	NX-C	VB	†

Took off with Sgt J. Gray at 15.25 for a calibration test. At 15.30 as a result of a special message from No.11 Group, Tangmere control warned them to be on the look out for bandits. The enemy aircraft were located 30 miles South East of Selsey Bill, Sussex. Shortly afterwards, one of the two pilots who could not be identified said they were under attack from Fw190s. Nothing else was heard from either of the two pilots. At 17.00, four Spitfires took off to search the area without results. Davidson had received his commission by that time (J.16056) but had still to acknowledge his notification. John Davidson, native from Ontario, Canada, had joined the squadron in July 1942.
Note on the aircraft: Presentation aircraft 'CANTERBURY'. TOC No.37 MU 27.07.41, issued to No.131 Sqn 20.08.42 after having served with Nos.485 (NZ) and 134 Sqns.

	Sgt James **GRAY**		RAF No.975279	RAF	**BM472**		VB	†

See above. James Gray of Bexley Heath, Kent, had joined the squadron two months previously.
Note on the aircraft: TOC No.37 MU 12.04.42, issued to No.131 Sqn date unrecorded but had served with the USAAF (308th FS) until 12.09.42.First trace in 131 ORB, 15.09.42.

11.11.42   P/O Emrys A.J. **WILLIAMS**   RAF No.117304   RAF   **AA719**   NX-S   VB   †

At 11.19, the squadron took off on an offensive patrol to a point 15 miles off the Somme estuary. All 12 aircraft went across at sea level, and when about 15-20 miles off the French coast, two aircraft of Red section went up to 6,000 feet as a decoy for enemy fighters while the rest of the squadron orbited at sea level. The patrol was uneventful but on the way home, 'Taffy' Williams collided in cloud with the aircraft flown by S/Lt Bernard Scheidhauer (FFAF), crashing south of Shoreham. 'Taffy' Williams of Chorlton-cum-Hardy, Manchester, was due to go on leave the same evening to see his wife and his son, who had been born the evening before. Williams had joined the squadron in May. (see also accident 19.05.42).

Note on the aircraft: TOC No.5 MU 08.09.41, issued to No.131 Sqn 10.10.42. Served previously with Nos.306 (Polish), 303 (Polish) and 616 Sqns.

            S/Lt Bernard W.M. **SCHEIDHAUER**   F.30649   FFAF   **EN889**   VB   -

See above. S/Lt Scheidhauer, a student when France collapsed in June 1940, had come to the UK in October 1940 and served with No.242 (Canadian) Sqn before being posted to 131 Squadron when No. 242 was sent to Malta. Shot down and made PoW the following month.

Note on the aircraft: TOC No.37 MU 13.05.42, issued to No.131 Sqn 27.10.42. Served previously with No.340 (French) Sqn.

18.11.42   S/Lt Bernard W.M. **SCHEIDHAUER**   F.30649   FFAF   **EN830**   NX-G   VB   **PoW**

Two Rhubarb missions were planed that day. In the first, Bernard Scheidhauer took off as No.2 to S/Lt de Bordas (FFAF) at 14.10 for Caen and Cherbourg. They crossed the Channel at sea level and made French landfall at St-Aubin-sur-Mer. They then flew Westward along the Caen-Cherbourg railway, avoiding Bayeux, on through Carentan, and out again opposite Ecousseville, keeping almost at ground level all the time. Scheidhdauer attacked a locomotive at Carentan and damaged it seriously while S/Lt de Bordas attacked three locos between Bayeux and Airel, and one beyond Carentan. Two others were claimed as damaged. A certain amount of light flak was experienced from Carentan and from one flak post between Bayeux and Airel. Just before turning East at Econsville, de Bordas lost sight of his wingman. Scheidhauer was actually hit by flak near Ouistream and crashed on Jersey. Later reported as a PoW at Stalag Luft III, he was executed by the Gestapo during the 'Great Escape'.

Note on the aircraft: Presentation aircraft 'CHILSEHURST & SIDCUP'. TOC No.37 MU 01.05.42, issued to No.131 Sqn 08.06.42. Aircraft capture almost intact by the Germans and re-used.

            Sgt Edward **APPLETON-BACH**   RAF No.1378956   RAF   **X4342**   VB   †

In the second Rhubarb, Sgt Appleton-Bach took off as No.2 to P/O H.S. Jackson at 14.15, heading for Ouistream. They flew at sea level, crossing the French coast west of Ouistream before sweeping inland behind the town and coming out again along the canal. On his return Jackson reported successful attacks on one loco, the boiler of which exploded, one of a group of five oil storage tanks left with smoke pouring from it, and a burst directed at masted vessels along the canal banks. On the way back when crossing Ouistream, they were met by intense accurate light flak from the town and harbour. Jackson's aircraft was hit in the wing by an explosive shell. Sgt Appleton-Bach was hit in his port side and consequently passed nearer the centre of the town. Jackson lost sight of him and saw sheet of flames from the town, thinking that it was Appleton-Bach's aircraft. Doll took off on a search for the two missing pilots without results. Appleton-Bach had joined the squadron the previous month.

Note on the aircraft: Built as Mk.IB and TOC 08.09.40 and served with No.19 Sqn. Converted to Mk.VB and served with No.92 Sqn, No.316 (Polish) Sqn, 154 and 121 (Eagle), 340 (French) Sqns before to be issued to No.131 Sqn 27.10.42.

30.06.43   F/Sgt John L. **CHANDLER**   NZ415407   RNZAF   **AB504**   VC   †

The squadron was called upon to provide various convoy escort and patrols that day. At 09.45 F/Sgt Chandler took off with F/Sgt P.H. Clatworthy to escort merchant vessels South of Plymouth. After escorting the patrol for one hour, while flying line abreast at 400-500 feet near Eddystone Lighthouse, Chandler was heard to tell to his No.2 that he was experiencing engine trouble. He then lost height rapidly, and Clatworthy saw Chandler ditching one mile South of the lighthouse. The Spitfire's tail remained visible for three seconds before sinking. The Walrus sent later didn't find anything. Chandler had joined the squadron in February, and was the first operational loss for seven months. He had previously survived being torpedoed while en route to the UK. His brother Edward had lost his life while serving No.485 Sqn the previous year, in April 1942.

Note on the aircraft: Served as test aircraft before being issued to No.131 Sqn 04.05.43.

03.08.43   F/O Eearl R. **SMITH**   Aus.405894   RAAF   **EP614**   VB   **PoW**

The squadron (12 aircraft) took off with Exeter Wing at 19.25 for Circus 49 to escort Whirlwinds targeting Brest aerodrome, F/L T.G. Pickering leading the squadron. Shortly after the beginning of the return journey, around 12 enemy fighters were sighted,

which engaged 131 Squadron. F/Sgt Parry was able to claim a probable Fw190 and the CO, P/O Luckhoff, F/Sgt Turnbull and F/Sgt Tate each made claims of enemy aircraft damaged (Luckoff claimed two). Earl Smith was posted missing, having last been heard reporting that he had been hit by Fw190s. Later reported as a PoW at Stalag Luft III. Earl Smith was native of New South Wales, Australia, and had joined the squadron in April 1943 after having served with No.165 Sqn between February and April 1943.
Note on the aircraft: TOC No.39 MU 05.07.42. Served with Nos.313 (Czech) and 310 (Czech) Sqns before being issued to No.131 Sqn 02.07.43.

| 18.08.43 | F/O Cyril B. SMITH | Aus.405886 | RAAF | AR506 | VC | PoW |

Took off at 0945 with 10 others for Ramrod 208 to Woendrecht (Holland), the CO leading, and the Squadron flying with 504 Sqn. Smith reported engine trouble at 12,000 feet over the target and was seen diving steeply away, before crash-landing near Woensdrecht. Later reported as a PoW at Stalag Luft IV. Cyril Smith was an Australian from New South Wales, and had joined the squadron in December 1942.
Note on the aircraft: TOC No.38 MU 25.06.42, issued to No.131 Sqn 02.07.43. Served previously with 310 (Czech) Sqn.

| 19.08.43 | F/Sgt Robert K. PARRY | RAF No.1379966 | RAF | AR371 | VB | - |

At 16.25 in the evening, the squadron took off on Ramrod 210 for the close escort of Marauders bombing Byas-Sud aerodrome near St-Pol (France), with the CO leading the 11 aircraft. On the way back at 12,000 feet, six Fw190s coming from the Boulogne direction bounced Yellow section. Soon Parry's aircraft was hit on the port wing and fuselage and his aircraft caught fire. He managed to keep his aircraft straight and level and flew it two-thirds of the way back over the Channel, baled out off Dungeness and was subsequently picked up by a vessel of the Dover patrol. Robert Parry had joined the squadron in October 1942.
Note on the aircraft: TOC No.38 MU 14.03.42, issued to No.131 Sqn 20.07.43. Served previously with No.303 (Polish) Sqn and FAA.

| 27.08.43 | P/O Francis W. BATEMAN | RAF No.52433 | RAF | EE768 | VC | † |

Took off at 0740 with eleven others for an escort of US B-26s (Ramrod S.6) to Rouen, the CO leading. Near the target, around 20 enemy aircraft attacked the formation from the North and East. Two Spitfires were seen going down near the target West of Queville (France), Bateman's aircraft being one of them. He had been with the squadron since January 1943.
Note on the aircraft: TOC No.38 MU 01.12.42, issued to No.131 Sqn 11.01.43. Then served with Nos.412 (RCAF), 421 (RCAF) and 310 (Czech) Sqns before returning to the squadron.

| | F/Sgt Guy F. ANDREWS | RAF No.1387467 | RAF | EP547 | VB | PoW |

See above. Andrews had joined the squadron recently in June. He was later reported as a PoW at Dulag Luft.
Note on the aircraft: TOC No.9 MU 03.07.42. Served Nos.312 (Czech) and 310 (Czech) Sqns before being issued to No.131 Sqn 02.07.43.

| 04.09.43 | 1st Lt Franklin D. BURT | O-660240 | USAAF | EE746 | VC | † |

Took off at 16.50 with 10 other for Ramrod S.31, an escort to Marauders bombing Lille marshalling yards, in company with the Redhill Wing. On the return journey, Yellow section was jumped by four Fw190s, five miles North of Dunkirk. Aircraft was hit by Fw190s in the ailerons. Pilot turned 90° and levelled out into a shallow dive towards the French coast. He dived into the Channel just east of Dunkirk (France). American pilot attached from 12th RS/67th RG in July 1943 for operational training. MACR 0548.
Note on the aircraft: TOC No.38 MU 26.11.42. issued to No.131 Sqn 21.12.42. Then served with Nos.412 (RCAF), 421 (RCAF) and 310 (Czech) Sqns before returning to the squadron 02.07.43.

| 08.09.43 | Sgt Eric N. DALBY | RAF No.1676158 | RAF | AB282 | VB | - |

Engine failure following take off at 15.28 for Circus S.41 (an escort to 12 Venturas to bomb Abbeville marshalling yards). The pilot believed he could reach the airfield and lowered the undercarriage and flaps but fell short and force-landed hitting a hedge, Crab Tree Lane, one mile South East of Redhill, Surrey. He had joined the squadron in June 1943 and left in May 1944.
Note on the aircraft: TOC No.8 MU 05.01.42, issued to No.131 Sqn 03.07.43 after having served with Nos.611 and 242 Sqns.

20.12.43   F/Sgt Arthur F. **Tate**   NZ415387   RNZAF   **MA224**   IX   -

F/Sgt Tate had taken off at 9.30 with F/Sgt R. Cross (RAAF) for a convoy escort. Around 11.00, returning from the flight, the engine cut out at 1000 feet and emitted clouds of black smoke. Tate attempted to make a wheels-up landing three and a half miles East of Exeter. Tate had joined the squadron in February 1943, and returned in January 1944 upon the recovery of slight injuries sustained during the force-landing. However he left the following month at the end of his tour.

Note on the aircraft: Served first with No.340 (French) Sqn on 11.05.43 then with No.222 Sqn before being issued to No.131 sqn 27.09.43.

23.04.44   W/O Douglas F. **Philipps**   Aus.401394   RAAF   **MB935**   NX-Z   VII   †

Took off at 17.00 on scramble with W/O C.J. Crayford. Lost contact with his wingman and crashed into the sea 25 miles off Bolt Head. An Australian native of Ireland, Philipps served in various second line units in the Middle East and UK before joined the squadron in December 1943.

Note on the aircraft: TOC No.39 MU 15.02.44, issued to No.131 Sqn 26.02.44.

17.05.44   F/Sgt Jeffrey E. **Morris**   RAF No.1390161   RAF   **MD166**   VII   **Eva.**

Led by F/L Moody (RCAF), four Spitfires took off at 05.45 for a shipping reconnaissance. Two minesweepers were seen near Lizardrieux and attacked. Believing he had been hit by flak, Morris made an emergency landing 16 km South West of Lannion but was trapped under his Spitfire and eventually captured by German soldiers. Sent to Paris, he managed to escape after arriving there on the 18th when he was taking the Metro. He was hidden in Paris until 28th August when the city was liberated. Morris had served with the Squadron since March 1943.

Note on the aircraft: TOC No.39 MU 04.01.44, issued to No.131 Sqn date unrecorded.

01.06.44   W/O Wiliam J. **Atkinson**   Aus.413332   RAAF   **MB887**   VII   †

Led by F/L de Burgh, eight Spitfires took off at 11.40 for Rhubarb 265, and flew at sea level to cross the French coast at St Brienne Bay. They remained together until reaching Lamballe then split into two formations of four, one turning West, the another turning East. W/O Atkinson was No.4 in the formation turning West led by F/O Catterall, which continued to fly at ground level. At 12.30, South West of St-Bruec, they saw a goods train of about 15 trucks moving West slowly. The attack was ordered but when the flight reformed, Atkinson was not there. It is believed he had been shot down by flak. A native of New South Wales, Australia, he served as a flying instructor, before joining the Squadron in December 1943.

Note on the aircraft: TOC No.39 MU 07.02.44, issued to No.131 Sqn 03.03.44.

07.06.44   W/O Jack E. **Woodey**   Aus.411625   RAAF   **MB883**   VII   †

Posted missing from Rhubarb 272. Australian native of New South Wales, he served as flying instructor before joining operational units, No.453 (RAAF) Sqn between September and November 1943, No.276 Sqn between January and April 1944 and then No. 131 Squadron in April.

Note on the aircraft: TOC No.39 MU 30.01.44, issued to No.131 Sqn 24.02.44.

12.06.44   F/L Vincent K. **Moody**   Can./J15362   RCAF   **MD123**   VII   †

Twelve aircraft took off at 13.00 with 12 Spitfire VIIs of 616 Squadron for Rodeo 169. Shot down by Fw190 near Le Mans, Moody was seen going to a steep climb just after crossing the airfield and was heard to say he was going to bale out. An American-born Canadian of Nova Scotia parents, 'Junior' Moody had served overseas since August 1941, first posted to No.118 Sqn before being posted to Malta the following Spring. He served with No.249 Sqn and returned to the UK in October with one confirmed victory to his credit. He started a second tour of operations during Autumn 1943 with No.610 Sqn with which he claimed his second and last kill on 8th October. He had served with the squadron since February 1944. [DFC No.610 Sqn] .

Note on the aircraft: TOC No.33 MU 01.01.44, issued to No.131 Sqn 29.02.44.

          F/O James S. **Hannah**   Can./R.99388   RCAF   **MD128**   VII   -

See above. On landing after this operation, the mainplane bulcked due to evasive action. The aircraft was later Struck Off Charge (SOC) the following September. A native of New Brunswick, Canada, Hannah was sent overseas in March 1942. His first operational posting seems to have been 501 Sqn in September 1942. He joined 131 Sqn in April 1944, posted from No.276 Sqn with which he had served since Spring 1943. He was commissioned in August 1944. Repatriated to Canada in January 1945, he returned to the UK two months later. He was repatriated a second time in March 1946 and served with the RCAF between 1951 and 1958.

Note on the aircraft: TOC No.39 MU 08.01.44, issued to No.131 Sqn 22.05.44.

14.06.44   ?   **MD172**   VII   -

Reported to have been damaged on operations that day, but no details are available in the Operations Record Book (ORB) and no trace of operations are recorded for this aircraft on this date.
<u>Note on the aircraft</u>: TOC No.33 MU 14.03.44, issued to No.131 Sqn 07.04.44.

21.06.44   F/Sgt Ernest J. **TANNER**   RAF No.1323017   RAF   **MD131**   VII   -

At 17.45 W/O Croydon and F/Sgt Tanner were sent on a shipping recce to St-Peter Port. While approaching from the South, they found 10/10 cloud at 500 feet, and on leaving this they flew North, but ran into accurate and intense flak from the harbour area which hit Tanner's aircraft. He was able, however, to continue the journey but the engine cut on approach at Bolt Head and the Spitfire crashed, the pilot escaping injuries. Tanner had joined the Squadron two weeks before.
<u>Note on the aircraft</u>: TOC No.39 MU 20.01.44, issued to No.131 Sqn 07.03.44.

30.09.44   F/O John R. **BAXTER**   AUS.419922   RAAF **MD119**   VII   **Inj.**

Australian pilot from Victoria. Pilot reported a sudden loss of oil pressure between Gant and Antwerpen at around 18.15 when the Squadron was on the way home. Admitted to RAF Hospital Wroughton on 6th October 1944, suffering from concussion, and contusion of the knee. He had joined the Squadron in June and upon recovery was posted to No.453 (RAAF) Sqn in April 1945. He left for repatriation in November, and served post-war with the RAAF as O-33449.
<u>Note on the aircraft</u>: TOC No.33 MU 24.12.43, issued to No.131 Sqn 26.02.44.

Total: 28

APPENDIX VI
AIRCRAFT LOST IN ACCIDENTS

Date	Pilot		S/N	Origin	Serial	Mark	Fate

SPITFIRE

27.07.41   Sgt Stephen H. **VAVASOUR-DURRELL**   RAF No.1257744   RAF   **X4662**   IA   †

Sgt Durrell had taken off for an aerobatics flight when the starboard wing came off at about 1000 feet and the plane crashed one mile North of Northallerton, Yorks. Sydney Durrell had joined the squadron early that month.
<u>Note on the aircraft</u>: TOC No.9 MU 08.11.40, issued to No.131 Sqn 17.07.41. Served previously with No.485 (NZ) Sqn and No.61 OTU.

19.09.41   Sgt David F. **ROULEAU**   CAN/R.54206   RCAF **X4916**   IA   -

Returning from a practice scramble, the undercarriage collapsed upon landing on a rough surface combined with a strong cross-wind. The accident occurred at 14.50. David Rouleau was a Canadian from Ontario who had joined the Squadron in July. He remained with the Squadron until May 1942 when he volunteered to serve overseas and left with a commission. Embarking on HMS Eagle, he took off on 03.06.42 in a Spitfire (BR358) bound for Malta but was intercepted by Bf109s of II./JG53, shot down and killed.
<u>Note on the aircraft</u>: Presentation aircraft 'CITY OF HULL I'. TOC No.9 MU 03.01.41, issued to No.131 Sqn 02.09.41. Served previously with No.485 (NZ) Sqn.

28.09.41   P/O Henri A. **PICARD**   RAF No.87693   (BEL)/RAF **AR218**   IA   -

On 27 September, 21 officers and 117 airmen had proceeded by air and road from Ternhill to Atcham with Squadron equipment. Among 25 aircraft, there were 17 Spitfires and one Magister held by the Squadron. The following day, in the middle of afternoon, the whole party began to make the journey back when, on take-off from Atcham, P/O Picard in AR218 collided with Magister R1977 on the ground. Picard escaped major injuries, but the two pilots on board the Magister were killed (see later for further details). Henri Picard was a Belgian pilot who was a former regular Belgian Army officer. He switched to the Air Force in 1938 to train as an observer and in January 1940 he commenced a course to become a pilot. Still under training when the German laun ched their offensive in May 1940, he was evacuated to France and then to French Morocco, from whence he sailed to the UK. He completed his training with the RAF and was posted to the Squadron in August 1941. In November, he joined the newly-formed No.350 (Belgian) Sqn with which he served until being wounded in action on 27th August 1942. Shot down by Fw190s, he had to bale out over the sea and spent five days and nights in his dinghy. He was washed ashore on the French coast and after reco very in a military hospital, was sent to a PoW camp (Stalag Luft III). He participated in the 'Great Escape' of March 1944 and was among those executed by the Gestapo. He is known to have shot down three German aircraft, one being shared.

Note on the aircraft: TOC No.5 MU 30.08.41, issued to No.131 Sqn 17.09.41.

19.10.41   F/L Henri A.C. **Gonay**   RAF No.81635   (BEL)/RAF   **P7422**   IIA   -

F/L Gonay took off at 14.05 for a weather test, and was obliged to make a forced landing on a beach near the Golf Course at Prestatyn, North Wales owing to lack of petrol. He escaped injury. Henri Gonay was a pre-war military Belgian pilot who fled to the UK from France in June 1940. He was quickly re-trained and posted to No.235 Sqn in August during the Battle of Britain. In October, he left the unit to become a flying instructor and returned to the front line unit in August 1941 when he joined No.123 Sqn, then No.131 in September to lead the Belgian Flight of the Squadron. In November he was posted to No.350 (Belgian) Sqn upon its formation. In April 1942 he was posted to No.232 Sqn, and in August to No.129 Sqn to become its CO. In November 1942 his tour ended, and after a rest period, he returned to combat for another tour, being posted to No.263 Sqn in February 1944 as CO. On 14 June 1944, while leading the unit, his Typhoon (MN661) was hit by flak, crash-landed and a hit farmhouse in Grantez, Jersey. He was awarded the DFC the following month.

Note on the aircraft: TOC No.6 MU 16.09.40, first served with Nos.19 and 234 Sqns. Issued to No.131 Sqn 12.10.41.

23.10.41   Sgt David A.E. **Bremner**   Can./R.71701   RCAF   **P8546**   IIA   †

David Bremner was returning from an air-to-air firing exercise when he lost power and stalled on approach, diving into the ground at 10.40 at Tryddyn near Wrexham. A Canadian from Ontario, he had joined the squadron in July.

Note on the aircraft: TOC No.12 MU 23.06.41, issued to No.131 Sqn 12.10.41. Served previously with Nos.403 (RCAF)& 54 Sqns.

22.11.41   Sgt Clive R. **Briggs**   Aus.403011   RAAF   **P7560**   IIA   -

During a flying exercise, the pilot encountered bad visibility and was unable to obtain instructions via R/T. He pulled the control column back and opened full throttle to avoid a hill, but the aircraft spun out of control and the pilot baled out at 16.00. The aircraft crashed near Dale Head Farm, Hapur Hill, Derbysh. An Australian from New South Wales, he had joined the Squadron the previous month. He served with the Squadron until August 1942 and was repatriated to Australia. He was posted to No.457 (RAAF) Sqn in December 1942 for another tour he completed in August 1943. He never flew again in operations and served as flying instructor until the end of the war. He was commissioned and survived the war.

Note on the aircraft: TOC No.38 MU 25.10.40, issued to No.131 Sqn 01.10.41. Served previously with No.19 Sqn.

07.12.41   Sgt Horace A. **Metcalfe**   Aus.402962   RAAF   **P7746**   IIA   †

The accident occurred at 11.46 while practising camera gun and formation flying. Caught in a snowstorm, the pilot was unable to land and eventually stalled avoiding high ground near Rushton Cottage, The Wrekin, Salop. A native of New South Wales Australia, he had been posted to the Squadron the previous month.

Note on the aircraft: TOC No.9 MU 07.12.40, issued to No.131 Sqn 02.10.41. Served previously with Nos.403 (RCAF) and 54 Sqns.

10.03.42   P/O Harold A. **O'Blenes**   Can./J.15122   RCAF   **AB242**   VB   †

Flew into water tower while low flying over Llanbdr. Harold O'Blenes was a Canadian from New Brunswick who had served in the Squadron since January.

Note on the aircraft: TOC No.6 MU 27.11.41, issued to No.131 Sqn 10.12.41.

23.03.42   Sgt Roy K. **BRIDLE**   Aus.404675   RAAF   **BL411**   VB   -
Bridle took off at 10.20 with W3602 (Sgt J.L Davidson - RCAF) for a formation flight when both collided 10 minutes after the take-off. Bridle had to bale out from his uncontrollable Spitfire. An Australian pilot from New South Wales, he had joined the Squadron in November 1941. Commissioned, he served the Squadron until October 1942 when he was sent to Australia to serve with No.452 (RAAF) Sqn, but that did not take place. He never flew again in operations. (See also accident 16.04.42).
Note on the aircraft: TOC No.37 MU 23.11.41, issued to No.131 Sqn 10.12.41.

02.04.42   P/O David L.G. **TURVEY**   Can./J.7424   RCAF   **AB137**   VB   -
At 16.30, P/O Turvey was taxiing before a practice flight when the aircraft hit a lorry parked on the perimeter, because of lack of visibility. The pilot had decided not to wait for airmen on wing-tips to guide him to the runway. 'Topsy' Turvey, a Canadian from Ontario had just arrived at the Squadron. (See accident 03.05.42 & 05.05.42).
Note on the aircraft: TOC No.38 MU 27.11.41, issued to No.131 Sqn 11.12.41.

16.04.42   Sgt Roy K. **BRIDLE**   Aus.404675   RAAF   **BL433**   VB   -
Undercarriage was not fully locked while on landing at Llanbedr and the aircraft tipped on its nose. (See 23.03.42 – accident for details on the pilot).
Note on the aircraft: TOC No.24 MU 01.12.41, issued to No.131 Sqn 09.01.42.

18.04.42   Sgt Alan W. **BOWER**   RAF No.778642   (SA)/RAF **W3700**   VB   -
Sgt Bower had taken off for a local flight at 13.45 when he had to face an engine failure. The pilot had limited choice of suitable fields and made a wheels-up landing five miles East of Criccieth, Caernarvon. Unfortunately one wing of the aircraft hit a tree causing irreparable damage to the aircraft. The pilot escaped injury. 'Bill' Bower had first joined the SAAF when the War broke out but transferred to the RAF a couple of weeks later to be able to fight in Europe. In March 1942 he briefly served with No.134 Sqn before joining No.131 Sqn, where he served until February 1943. Later that year he served with No.234 Sqn between June and November 1943. In May 1944 he was posted to No.33 Sqn to commence a second tour and early in 1945 he joined No.222 Sqn as Flight Commander. He stayed a short time with the latter before being posted back to No.33 Sqn in March, as CO, where he remained until July 1946. He was credited with three confirmed victories, two being shared. In the post-war years he continued to serve with the RAF until 1967. [DFC No.33 Sqn].
Note on the aircraft: TOC No.45 MU 25.08.41, issued to No.131 Sqn 09.01.42.

03.05.42   P/O David L.G. **TURVEY**   Can./J.7424   RCAF   **BL371**   VB   -
On return to Llanbedr from a night practice flight, the pilot made a heavy landing at 23.55, after having levelled off too high, and opened the throttle too late to prevent the aircraft stalling. The undercarriage collapsed and the Spitfire was too damaged to be repairable. For Turvey, it was his second accident in a month (see accident 02.04.42 and 05.05.42).
Note on the aircraft: TOC No.37 MU 27.11.41, issued to No.131 Sqn 10.12.41.

05.05.42   P/O David L.G. **TURVEY**   Can./J.7424   RCAF   **R7337**   VB   -
Two days later, 'Topsy' Turvey was airborne for an Army Co-Operation flight. The pilot returned to Llanbedr but failed to check if the undercarriage was down and locked. Turvey landed at 19.00 with undercarriage unlocked, with disastrous consequences for the aircraft and also for the pilot, who was withdrawn from operations to undertake further training having wrecked three Spitfires in one month. By the end of the year he was dispatched to the Middle East with No.92 sqn, then No.417 (RCAF) Sqn. When he was sent home in October 1944, he had shot down two enemy aircraft and had become a Flight Commander with No.417 Sqn. He was released from active service in May 1945.
Note on the aircraft: Served as test aircraft before being issue to an operational unit (452, 602 & 41 Sqns). Issue to No.131 Sqn 13.05.42.

11.05.42   P/O Keith A.H. **MASON**   RAF No.111704   RAF   **BL317**   VB   -
P/O Mason had taken off with another Spitfire of the Squadron for a formation flight when at 15.45 the engine of his Spitfire overheated and failed due to loss of coolant. He belly-landed on a beach, Ton fannau, eight miles South of Barmouth, Merioneth. Unfortunately the aircraft struck a rock and was too badly damaged to be repairable. He left the Squadron in August having volunteered to serve in Middle East, where he served with No.253 Sqn. [DFC No.253 Sqn].
Note on the aircraft: TOC No.37 MU 23.11.41, issued to No.131 Sqn 10.12.41.

19.05.42   P/O Emrys A.J. **Williams**   RAF No.117304   RAF   **P8445**   VB   -

Williams had taken off for a sector recce when on returning at 11.00, he made a heavy landing at Merston and the port oleo leg collapsed. He was later killed on operations (see 11.11.42).

Note on the aircraft: Built as a Mk.IIA. TOC No.9 MU 15.06.41, served with No.122 Sqn before convertion to a Mk.VB. Issued to No.131 Sqn 14.04.42.

01.03.43   S/L John S. **Fifield**   RAF No.83274   RAF   **BL659**   VB   -

S/L Fifield took off at 14.50 to practise aerobatics. The engine cut, and he ditched five miles East of Wick. He had previously flown with Nos.602 and 616 Sqns in 1942, before being posted to the squadron as CO. In March 1943 he completed his tour, but returned to operational duty at the end of the year with No.169 Sqn, flying Mosquitoes, with which he was later awarded a DFC. His claims consisted of two confirmed victories, and one probable. He remained with the RAF after the war.

Note on the aircraft: TOC No.39 MU 06.02.42, issued to No.131 Sqn 25.01.43. Served previously with Nos.130 & 610 Sqns.

01.12.43   F/Sgt William E. **Wood**   RAF No.1083972   RAF   **MA799**   IX   †

At first light the Squadron took off to fly to Ford as a forward base for Ramrod 343. The formation ran into thick cloud after a few minutes flying, and while circumventing a range of hills, F/Sgt Wood was seen diving into ground and crashed six miles North of Blandford, Dorset. He had served with the squadron since July.

Note on the aircraft: TOC direct to No.129 Sqn 17.07.43. Issued to No.131 Sqn 27.09.43.

04.02.44   W/O Alfred S. **Arnold**   RAF No.915438   RAF   **MA860**   IX   †

On this day the Wing was sent from Ford to Tangmere and from there to Hawkinge. Largely due to the crosswind and the soft state of the airfield, Arnold's Spitfire swung round almost into a down-wind position as soon as he touched down. He attempted to take off again and go around, but failed to clear a bank on the aerodrome boundary. The undercarriage hit a hedge and the aircraft overturned and caught fire. The pilot was extricated quickly and taken to Canterbury Hospital with severe burns. He died the following day. Arnold had joined the squadron in September 1943.

Note on the aircraft: TOC No.33 MU 21.08.43. Issued to No.131 Sqn 27.09.43.

25.08.44   F/L Cecil E. **Bearman**   RAF No.122343   RAF   **MD171**   VII   †

At 09.00, eleven aircraft took of from Manston to for Culmhead led by Wing Commander Brothers. Thick cloud was encountered near Salisbury and F/L 'Tete' Bearman leading Blue section during a climb through cloud, apparently lost control and dived straight into the ground near Old Sarum. 'Tete' Bearman had served with the Squadron since September 1943.

Note on the aircraft: TOC No.33 MU 14.03.44. Issued to No.131 Sqn 17.06.44.

21.03.45   W/O John B. **Wingate**   RAF No.163142   RAF   **MV126**   VIII   -

W/O Hioward Jones was taxiing in MT881 to the take-off position at Amarda Road airfield to take part in a cine gun exercise when he struck MV126 which was waiting its turn to take off. Nobody was hurt but MV126 were damaged enough to be stricken off charge - it is believed that it was repairable, but the end of war against Japan prompted this decision. MT881 was repaired.

Note on the aircraft: TOC No.9 MU 20.08.44. Sent Far East and arrived in India 04.11.44. Issued to No.131 Sqn, not recorded.

06.04.45   F/O Eric F. **Mitchell**   RAF No.181250   RAF   **JF827**   VIII   †

At 12.25 while taxiing over rough ground for a test flight from Amarda Road, the oleos of the main wheels entered mud and the aircraft tipped onto its nose. Mitchell was among the pilots who arrived at the Squadron in the Far East in February 1945. The aircraft had been damaged on 30 March by F/Sgt N. Langdon1575786 30.03.45 but the aircraft was repaired.

Note on the aircraft: TOC No.6 MU 18.08.43. Sent Far East and arrived in India 03.11.43. Issued to No.131 Sqn, not recorded.

07.06.45   F/Sgt William A. **Heslop**   RAF No.1333324   RAF   **JF276**   VIII   †

While undertaking a practice flight, the aircraft developed unspecified technical trouble and crashed. William Heslop was among the pilots who arrived with the Squadron in the Far East in February 1945.

Note on the aircraft: TOC No.33 MU 29.11.42. Shipped to India arriving 01.12.43. Issued to No.131 Sqn date unrecorded.

THUNDERBOLTS

02.10.45   W/O John H.F. **JAMES**   RAF No.1339604   RAF   **KL286**   II   †

The pilot was operating in poor visibility and with cloud base of 500 feet. While flying on instruments, it is believed that he lost control and dived into the ground near Zayatkwin. John James was a former No.134 Sqn pilot who had joined the Squadron in September 1944.

Note on the aircraft: Built as P-47D-30-RE 44-20845. Shipped to India in *S.S. Philander* 16.01.45, arriving 22.02.45.

31.10.45   F/O Jeffrey G. **HANSON**   RAF No.55136   RAF   **KL179**   II   †

Jeffrey Hanson was conducting an air test and encountered technical problem with the propeller's constant speed unit. He attempted to make a forced landing on the airfield (Kuala Lumpur) but overshot and decided to go round again. The throttle was opened but a small fire was seen in the area of the exhaust, and the aircraft lost height and crashed into a stream. Hanson was not a former No.134 Sqn and he should have joined No.131 Sqn during the summer.

Note on the aircraft: Built as P-47D-30-RE 44-20639. Shipped to India in *S.S. Ridgefield* 23.11.44, arriving 19.12.44.

MAGISTER

28.09.41   P/O Peter **CHUBB**   RAF No.65521   **R1977**   I   †
              Sgt Stanley D. **LEE**   RAF No.927861   †

Collided on take off with Spitfire AR218, at Ternhill (see AR218 for details). Both pilots were founder members of the Squadron.

Note on the aircraft: TOC No.9 MU 16.01.40. Isued No.131 Sqn 24.07.41.

Total: 26
including 25 combat aircraft

APPENDIX VII
Aircraft serial numbers matching with individual letters

NX-A
BM420 *(Spitfire V)*
MA834 *(Spitfire IX)*

NX-B
AD411 *(Spirfire V)*
MD183 *(Spitfire IX)*

NX-C
AD348 *(Spitfire V)*

NX-D
P7560 *(Spitfire II)*
AB364 *(Spitfire V)*

NX-E
AD425 *(Spitfire V)*

NX-F

NX-G
AB282, EN830 *(Spitfire V)*

NX-H
BL600 *(Spitfire V)*

NX-I

NX-J

NX-K
P7746 *(Spitfire II)*
AB142 *(Spitfire V)*

NX-L
X4179 *(Spitfire I)*
MD172 *(Spitfire VII)*

NX-M
P9306 *(Spitfire I)*
P7912 *(Spitfire II)*
MD165 *(Spitfire VII)*

NX-N

NX-O
MD120 *(Spitfire VII)*

NX-P
P8164 *(Spitfire II)*
BM632 *(Spitfire V)*
MD134 *(Spitfire VII)*

NX-Q
P8180 *(Spitfire II)*
BL769 *(Spitfire V)*
MD111 *(Spitfire VII)*

NX-R
P7352 *(Spitfire II)*
AB972 *(Spitfire V)*

NX-S
P9433 *(Spitfire I)*
P8776 *(Spitfire II)*
AA719 *(Spitfire V)*

NX-T

NX-U

NX-V
MD187 *(Spitfire VII)*

NX-W
AR378 *(Spitfire V)*

NX-X
BM121 *(Spitfire V)*
MD125 *(Spitfire VII)*

NX-Y

NX-Z
EN791 *(Spitfire V)*
MH852 *(Spitfire IX)*

APPENDIX VIII
LIST OF KNOWN PILOTS POSTED OR ATTACHED TO THE SQUADRON

FAA
T.G. **HARTSHORNE**
P.H. **LONDON**
W.H. **STEVENSON**

FFAF
H.L.L.F. DE **BORDAS**, F.30226
L. **GUILLOUX**, F.30127
F. **HORVATH**, F.30654
R.L. **LEGUIE**, F.30270
M. **LORAND**, F.30687
R.A. **SIMON**, F.30195
A.P.F. **VILBOUX**, F.30330
B.W.M. **SCHEIDHAUER**, F.30649
J.L.P.M.H. **STOURM**, F.30321

RAAF
A.G.H. **ARNOT**, Aus.402840
W.J. **ATKINSON**, Aus.413332
J.R. **BAXTER**, Aus.419922
R.K. **BRIDLE**, Aus.404675
C.R. **BRIGGS**, Aus.403011
F.W. **CLEWLEY**, Aus.400579
R.F. **CROSS**, Aus.413366
AV.N. **EDE**, Aus.405302
W.C. **FRANCIS**, Aus.404955
J.E. **FRANKS, Aus.403731
W.N. **GODFREY, Aus.412521
F.H. **GOULD, Aus.414671
F.D. **HAMILTON**, Aus.403050
J.C.L. **HENNING**, Aus.411494
D.E. **JOHNSTON**, Aus.412550
E.T.A. **JONES, Aus.423134
J.M. **LOCK**, Aus.404967
A.L. **LUMLEY**, Aus.411587
C.V. **MADIGAN**, Aus.40856
E.L. **MAHAR**, Aus.33231
F.P. **McNULTY**, Aus.420588
H.A. **METCALFE**, Aus.402962
K.R. **MITCHELL**, Aus.404928
J.D. **NEWICK**, Aus.403366
E.M. **OLDHAM**, Aus.402749
G.C.W. **O'NEIL**, Aus.403475
H.A. **PATTON**, Aus.414262
D.F. **PHILLIPS**, Aus.401394
A.T. **RUSTIN-ROWE**, Aus.411389
C.B. **SMITH**, Aus.405886
E.R. **SMITH**, Aus.405894
J.G.R. **SMITH**, Aus.405984
M. De. P. **SYKES**, Aus.407261
N.A.A. Turnbull-Smithellsl, Aus.408891
W.W. **WALDRON**, Aus.405252
J.R. **WILSON**, Aus.409264
J.E. **WOODEY**, Aus.41625

RAF
J.N. **ABRAMS, RAF No.196171
H.R. **ALLEN**, RAF No.42582
G.F. **ANDREWS**, RAF No.1387467
E. **APPLETON-BACH**, RAF No.1378956
A.S. **ARNOLD**, RAF No.915438
P.H. **AREND**, RAF No.102532, *BELGIUM*
A.W. **ARROWSMITH**, RAF No.1164962
D.G. **AXFORD, RAF No.1321775
A.S. **BANCROFT, RAF No.1534943
G.C. **BANNING-LOVER**, RAF No.40283
F.W. **BATEMAN**, RAF No.52433
C.E. **BEARMAN**, RAF No.122343
R.N. **BELGROVE**, RAF No.37902
A.M. **BENTLEY**, RAF No.33220
M.L.F. **BEYTAGH**, RAF No.39052
F.E.W. **BIRCHFELD**, RAF No.39777
S.P.V. **BIRD**, RAF No.70064
J.P. **BLACKMORE, RAF No.123096
H.B. **BLACKWELL-SMITH**, RAF No.1166749
N.D. **BOOKER, RAF No.136195
A. **BOUSSA**, RAF No.101465, *BELGIUM*
A.W. **BOWER**, RAF No.80435, *SOUTH AFRICA*
L.V.C. **BROOKER**, RAF No.1266376
L.E. **BROOKES**, RAF No.1333938
R.U.P DE **BURGH**, RAF No.118569
S.A. **CATARALL**, RAF No.149228
W.G. **CLARKSON, RAF No.1605786
P.H. **CLATWORTHY**, RAF No.1166709
P. **CHUBB**, RAF No.65521
R.A. **COOPER**, RAF No.591184
D.A. **COUTTES**, RAF No.1375929
I.K. **CRAWFORD**, RAF No.115189
C.J.V. **CRAYFORD**, RAF No.1260758
W.G. **CREEVY**, RAF No.125322
G.E. **CRUWYS**, RAF No.33510
R.J. **CUPIT**, RAF No.1167825
W.H.L. **CUSACK**, RAF No.1795427
R.F. van **DAALEN WETTERS**, RAF No.???, *NETHERLANDS*
E.N. **DALBY**, RAF No.1676158
G.F.M. **DELTOUR**, RAF No.100651, *BELGIUM*
I.A.J. **DENNAHY, RAF No.162826
J.C.L. **DOLL**, RAF No.87445
G.A.B. **EDWARDS**, RAF No.142070
L.G. **ESTER**, RAF No.1299910, *BELGIUM*
J.S. **FIFIELD**, RAF No.83274
F.F. **FINNIS**, RAF No.80035, *RHODESIA*
C.G. **FORD, RAF No.67659
K.R. **FOSKETT**, RAF No.169019
*J.R. **GRAHAM**, RAF No.116445
J. **GRAY**, RAF No.975279
A.M. **GRIFFITHS**, RAF No.1604458
H.A.C. **GONAY**, RAF No.81635, *BELGIUM*
D.A. **GUILLAUME**, RAF No.102953, *BELGIUM*

J.M. **HADOW**, RAF No.122121
B.M.G. DE **HAMPTINNE**, RAF No.82516, *BELGIUM*
G. **HANNAFORD**, RAF No.?
*J.G. **HANSON**, RAF No.55136
L.Y.G. **HARMEL**, RAF No.1299917, *BELGIUM*
R.W. **HARPER**, RAF No.?
*W.A. **HESLOP**, RAF No.1333324
B. **HIRST**, RAF No.169436
J. **HLADO**, RAF No.125414, *CZECHOSLOVAKIA*
C.G.S. **HODGKINSON**, RAF No.122361
A.C.W. **HOLLAND**, RAF No.83245
A. **HOPKINS**, RAF No.?
H.S. **JACKSON**, RAF No.63098
J.H.F. **JAMES, RAF No.1339604
*H. **JONES**, RAF No.1317823
G.F.J. **JONGBLOED**, RAF No.104592, *NETHERLANDS*
*K. **JONES**, RAF No.1419693
D.M. **KELBE**, RAF No.?
G.W. **KELLEY**, RAF No.?
E.H. **KING**, RAF No.41933
J.B. **KING**, RAF No.1397675, *ARGENTINA*
A.E. **KNAPP**, RAF No.?
T. **KRUML**, RAF No.83229, *CZECHOLOVAKIA*
*W.J. **LAIDLER**, RAF No.181250
S.D. **LEE**, RAF No.927861
R.G. **LEESON**, RAF No.1231272
*J.L. **LILBURN**, RAF No.156634
L. **LUCKHOFF**, RAF No.136931, *SOUTH AFRICA*
J. **LUXFORD**, RAF No.657635
I.N. **MacDOUGALL**, RAF No.33491
H.J. **MANN**, RAF No.42247
R.L.P. **MAINGARD**, RAF No.151561
D. **MALONE**, RAF No.1349745
K.A.H. **MASON**, RAF No.111704
L.R. **MASTERS, RAF No.1569189
E.G. **MATTA, RAF No.186739
E.A. **McCANN**, RAF No.1331773
X.L.A. **MENU**, RAF No.87683, *BELGIUM*
J.W. **MONK**, RAF No.101097, *USA*
R. **MILLER**, RAF No.1111811
*E.F. **MITCHELL**, RAF No.182250
*A. **MORGAN**, RAF No.1450638
J.E. **MORRIS**, RAF No.175271
F.R. **NEWMAN**, RAF No.1332397
D.E. **NICHOLSON**, RAF No.144387
P.A. **O'BRIEN**, RAF No.116764
J.J. **O'MEARA**, RAF No.40844
D. **PATTEN**, RAF No.119251
R.K. **PARRY**, RAF No.156786
M.J. **PLAS**, RAF No.87697, *BELGIUM*
H.A. **PAYZE**, RAF No.655513
H.A. **PICARD**, RAF No.87693, *BELGIUM*
T.G. **PICKERING**, RAF No.114471

A.H.A.F.V. **Plisnier**, RAF No.100654, *Belgium*
I.C. **Powell**, RAF No.1313994
A. **Pratt, RAF No.1622917
R.A. **Prince**, RAF No.69478
J.F.V.R. **de Puysseleyr**, RAF No.100652, *Belgium*
I.A. **Ratcliffe, RAF No.163052
F.W.T. **Read**, RAF No.1386383
A. **Reay**, RAF No.?
A.D. **Rigg**, RAF No.1380207
G. **Ricardo**, RAF No.149955
G.A. **Richards**, RAF No.125570
C.C. **Robertson, RAF No.1559282
A.E. **Robinson**, RAF No.39472, *Australia*
N.W. **Rowell**, RAF No.111130
C.P. **Rudland**, RAF No.65998
N.G.S. **Salter, RAF No.149936
R.W. **Sampson**, RAF No.116753
K. **Sayers**, RAF No.?
T.W. **Seddon**, RAF No.1086419
J.R. **Sergeant**, RAF No.?
G.H.M. **Seydel**, RAF No.1299926, *Belgium*
J.G. **Sleven, RAF No.1391259
C.A. **Smart**, RAF No.119226
R.S **Smets**, RAF No.87694, *Belgium*
*G.M. **Smith**, RAF No.134094
O. **Smik**, RAF No.130678, *Czechoslovakia*
J.A. **Sowrey**, RAF No.33551
W.R. **Steele**, RAF No.?
*J. **Stenton**, RAF No.47513
R.A. **Sutherland**, RAF No.41079
Tait, RAF No.?
*E.J. **Tanner**, RAF No.1323017
H. **Taylor**, RAF No.?
A. **Thomas, RAF No.657766
J.M. **Thompson**, RAF No.34183
J.D. **Thorogood**, RAF No.1293333
A. **Tofield**, RAF No.42324
A.R. **Tomlinson**, RAF No.1338070
S.H. **Vavasour-Durell**, RAF No.1257744
J.F. **Walden, RAF No.1317873
J.C.R. **Waterhouse**, RAF No.112749
G.E.H. **Watkins**, RAF No.1376183
P.R.W. **Wickham**, RAF No.33403
R. **de Wever**, RAF No.87692, *Belgium*
E.A.J. **Williams**, RAF No.117304
N.S. **Wilson**, RAF No.67105
*J.B. **Wingate**, RAF No.163942
E.B.H. **Woolley**, RAF No.123049

RCAF

D.A.E. **Bremner**, Can./R.71701
A.F. **Bunte**, Can./R.100604, *USA*
L.J. **Burke**, Can./R.72504
R.J. **Burrill**, Can./R.78700
A.A. **Carcary**, Can./R.86290
J.L. **Davidson**, Can./R.85602
A.F. **Eckert**, Can./J.15344, *USA*
R.E. **Evans**, Can./R.69234
P.E. **Etienne**, Can./J.15118
N.R. **Fowlow**, Can./J.15095

J.S **Hannah**, Can./R.99388
J.M. **Hemstock**, Can./J.23086
D. **Leslie**, Can./R.?
J.L. **Mitchell**, Can./R.71684
A.M. **Morrison**, Can R./56093
V.K. **Moody**, Can./J.15362
H.A. **O'Blenes**, Can./J.15122
G.G. **Ross**, Can./J.15345 *USA*
D.F. **Rouleau**, Can./J.15348
?? **Stewart**, Can./R.?
F.W. **Thomson**, Can./R.98144
D.L.G. **Turvey**, Can./J.7424

RNZAF

F.D. **Brown**, NZ404330
W.A. **Caldwell**, NZ416087
J.L. **Chandler**, NZ415407
H.G. **Copland**, NZ41469
W.H.F. **Dean**, NZ402857
L.G.R. **Donaldson**, NZ405241
B.B. **Davidson, NZ424074
C.W. **Elliott**, NZ41317
D.K. **MacDonald, NZ427297
J.V. **McIvor**, NZ402884
N.G. **Packard**, NZ405315
R.I. **Phillips**, NZ402893
B.J. **Ritchie**, NZ415363
A. **Roberts**, NZ421535
R.E. **Stout**, NZ2371
A.F. **Tate**, NZ415387
D. **Tyrrell-Baxter, NZ4213401
C.E.B. **Wood**, NZ414714
E.R. **Worts**, NZ405357

SAAF

R.R. **Aylward, SAAF No.329148V
D.D. **Deans, SAAF 328328V
G.K. **Sonderlund, SAAF No.328363V

USAAF

Avery
F.D. **Burt**, O-660240
Chilton
Dean
Morrison
Yate

*Former No.134 Sqn pilots
**Presence in Far East confirmed

APPENDIX IX
ROLL OF HONOUR
✝

Roll of Honour-Aircrew
No.131 Squadron

Name	Service No	Rank	Age	Origin	Date	Serial
APPLETON-BACH, Edward	RAF No.1378956	Sgt	27	RAF	18.11.42	X4342
ARNOLD, Alfred Stewart	RAF No.915438	W/O	25	RAF	05.02.44	MA860
ATKINSON, William James	AUS.413332	W/O	21	RAAF	01.06.44	MB887
BATEMAN, Francis Wilson	RAF No.52433	P/O	27	RAF	27.08.43	EE768
BEARMAN, Cecil Ernest	RAF No.122343	F/L	27	RAF	25.08.44	MD171
BREMNER, David Alexander Edward	CAN./R.71701	Sgt	21	RCAF	23.10.41	P8546
BURT, Franklin David	O-660240	1st Lt	*n/k*	USAAF	04.09.43	EE746
CHANDLER, John Lincoln	NZ415407	F/Sgt	22	RNZAF	30.06.43	AB504
CHUBB, Peter	RAF No.65521	P/O	*n/k*	RAF	28.09.41	R1977
DAVIDSON, John Lavery	CAN./R.85602	F/Sgt	22	RCAF	24.10.42	AB850
GRAY, James	RAF No.975279	Sgt	26	RAF	24.10.42	BM472
HANSON, Jeffrey Graydon	RAF No.55136	F/O	22	RAF	31.10.45	KL179
HESLOP, William Allan	RAF No.1333324	F/Sgt	*n/k*	RAF	07.06.45	JF276
JAMES, John Howard Frank	RAF No.1339604	W/O	24	RAF	02.10.45	KL286
LEE, Stanley Douglas	RAF No.927861	Sgt	21	RAF	28.09.41	R1977
LUXFORD, John	RAF No.657235	Sgt	22	RAF	15.08.42	AD554
METCALFE, Horace Albert	AUS.402962	Sgt	24	RAAF	07.12.41	P7746
MITCHELL, Eric Frank	RAF No.181250	F/O	23	RAF	06.04.45	JF827
MOODY, Vincent Kenneth	CAN./J.15362	F/L	24	RCAF	12.06.44	MD123
O'BLENES, Harold Albert	CAN./J.15122	P/O	20	RCAF	10.03.42	AB242
OLDHAM, Edward Murray	AUS.402749	Sgt	25	RAAF	27.03.42	AB249
PHILIPPS, Douglas Frederick*	AUS.401394	W/O	25	RAAF	24.04.44	MB935
ROWELL, Nathaniel William	RAF No.111130	P/O	*n/k*	RAF	05.06.42	BL250
SCHEIDHAUER, Bernard William Martial**	RAF F.30649	S/Lt	23	FFAF	25.03.44	-
VAVASOUR - DURRELL, Stephen Harold	RAF No.1257744	Sgt	24	RAF	27.07.41	X4662
WILLIAMS, Emrys Aloysius Joseph	RAF No.117304	P/O	23	RAF	11.11.42	AA719
WILSON, Neil Stewart	RAF No.67105	F/O	21	RAF	22.10.42	EN791
WOOD, William Eric	RAF No.1083972	F/Sgt	24	RAF	01.12.43	MA799
WOODEY, Jack Edward	AUS.411625	W/O	24	RAAF	07.06.44	MB883

*Irish-born Australian
**Died in capit

Total: 29

Australia: 5, Canada: 4, France: 1, New Zealand: 1, United Kingdom: 17, United States: 1

GROUNDCREW
NIL

n/k: not known

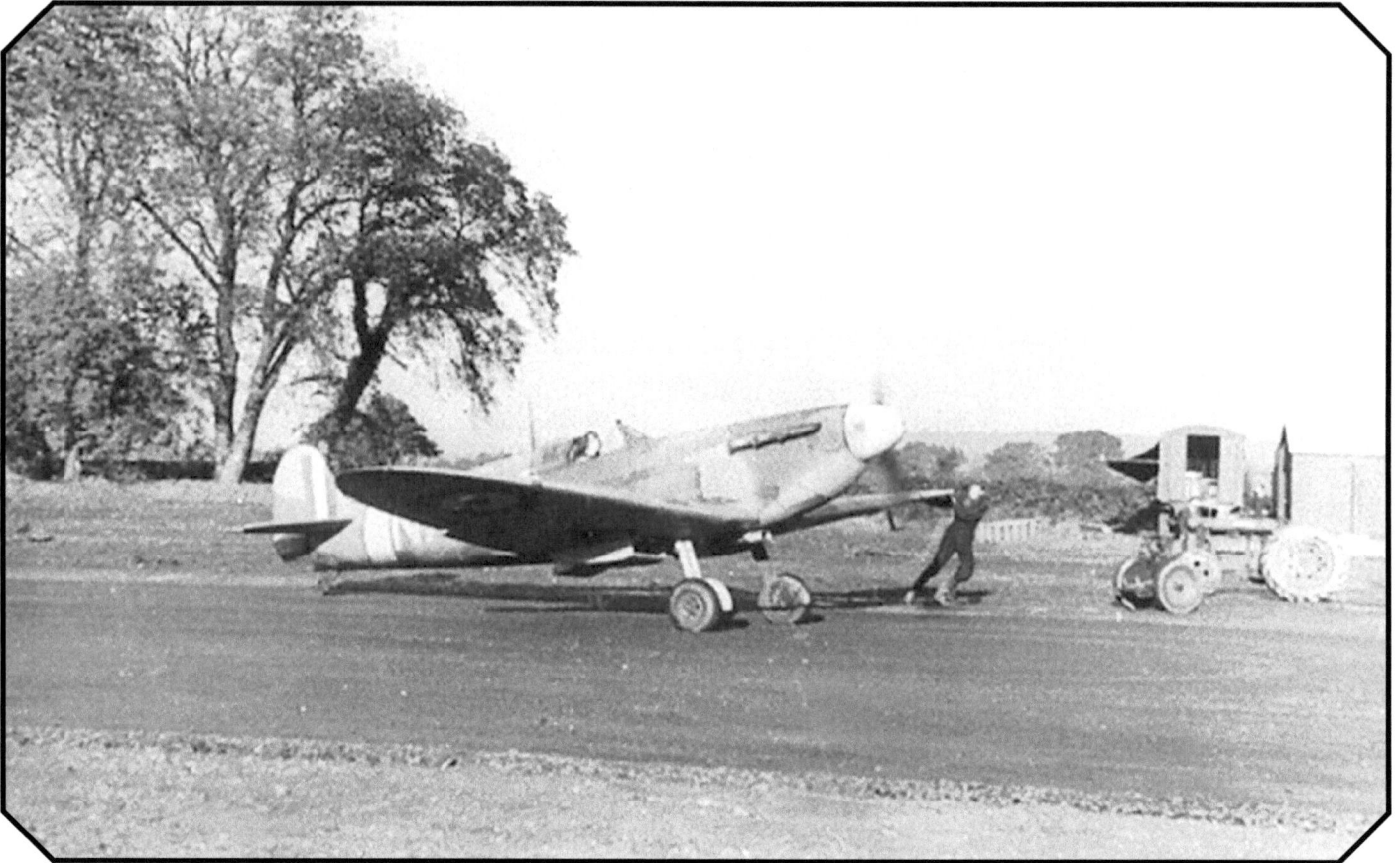

Like many RAF fighter squadrons raised in 1941 on Spitfires, the first model received was the ageing Mk.I, some aircraft being veterans of the Battle of Britain. Nevertheless, this allowed the young pilots another useful step after their weeks at OTUs. Below is P9306 of B (Belgian) Flight seen in October 1941 waiting for its pilot for another training flight. (*J.L. Roba via André Bar*)

Above, Spitfire Mk.I X4179/NX-L, of the Belgian flight, which was used by No.266 Sqn during the Battle of Britain. Below, Spitfire Mk.II P7746. The Mk.II was not intended to be the Squadron's official mount. Even with improved characteristics the Mk.II was at its very end of its operational career and had no real chance of success against the new Fw190 which was now in service with the Luftwaffe in Autumn 1941. (*J.L. Roba via André Bar*)

NNo.131 Squadron became really operational with the Spitfire Mk.V, the standard Spitfire version at that time. The Squadron was selected with some others as part of propaganda sequence to show Fighter Command in action during Spring 1942. The main reason was that this unit was composed of pilots coming from all the Empire and even beyond, including Americans and even French crews. These four pictures are also interesting as they show the slow introduction of the C3 roundel after 15.05.42. When the pictures were taken the new roundel had begun to be introduced and the Squadron was flying with a mixture of aircraft, with the old roundel still applied, the new roundel painted on at the factory, and the new roundel painted on the older ones. In the latter case, S/L Pedley's Spitfire is very representative the red colour painted on the white producing a kind of pink for the roundel and the fin flash - see colour profile. (*Andrew Thomas - above, Pedley's family via P. Sortahaug*)

Like most of the Spitfire squadrons of Fighter Command, No. 131 soldiered on with this version for a long time before transitioning onto the Mk.IX in September 1943, but this mark was kept for a short time only, less than six months. Above, AB142/NX-K served with the Squadron in the first half of 1943.

Left, one of the Mk.IXs in Squadron use in an uncomfortable position, for the pilot (P/O Stanley Catterall) at least, after the aircraft nosed over on the 04.02.44. The aircraft was repaired and continued to serve with other units later on. *(Andrew Thomas)*

Right, Spitfire Mk.IX MH852, usually flown by F/L C. Rudland early in 1944. Generaly speaking, the 131 made little use of the Mk.IX.

No.131 Squadron became somewhat unique when it converted to the Spitfire Mk.VII in Spring 1944. The Mk.VII was the first major re-design of the Spitfire and was dedicated to high level flying operations. Only 141 were built, hence only a couple of units became operational on the type, including No. 131. Most were delivered painted in Medium Sea Grey over PRU Blue camouflage and markings, but a handful received the standard Fighter Command camouflage and markings in service in 1944. MD183 was one of these. It is rather rare to get to see both sides of an aircraft, and the two shots show the elegant silhouette of the Spitfire Mk.VII. It is seen flying by the end of July 1944 when the D-Day bands have been partially deleted.

Taken on charge at No.39 MU on 15.02.44, MB935 was issued to No.131 Sqn 11 days later. It had received the paint scheme for high level flights. It was flown by various pilots, but it was the Irish-born Australian Douglas Phillips who was flying the aircraft when it was lost during a scramble on 23.04.44. Note that MB935 is wearing the standard camouflage for high altitude flight. However, as the photo shows, the codes letters were painted with outlined black paint which seems to have been discontinued later on.

(Paul Sortehaug)

Spitfire VII MD172 was taken on charge in April 1944 and was flown by various pilots. Comparing with MB983, the letters are not here outlined with black paint. Its final fate is not totally known, as it is stated that it was damaged in operations on 14.06.44 and re-categorised as beyond economic repair later on. However the ORB seems not to be reliable as MD172 doesn't appear in a Form 541 for that date, so the name of the pilot involved can't be determined. (*Andrew Thomas*)
MD120 (below) was one of the first Mk.VIIs to have been allocated to the Squadron, in February 1944. Another photo of this aircraft exists showing the Horse of Kent painted below the engine cowling, so we can imagine that it was still painted there when this photo was taken around D-Day, but unfortunately the angle of shot means that the wing is hiding the surface the Horse would be on. Note the D-Day markings have been crudely painted on the fuselage and wings. Despite a flying accident on 12.06.44, MD120 continued to serve the Squadron until the end of its association with that type. (*Andrew Thomas*)

Taken from various angle and time, Spitfire MD111 served with No.131 Sqn between February and October 1944. The two photos below are showing it somewhere at the end of July 1944 while the photo above was probably later in the summer, with various dirty marks around the engine and on the fuselage. The spinner seems to have been painted white by that time.

Squadron Leader Michael G.F. Pedley in 1942. He retired from the service in 1957 as a Group Captain, DSO, DFC, OBE.
(*Pedley family via P. Sortehaug*)

Michael G.F. Pedley became the first CO of No.131 Squadron to really bring the unit into combat. He was commissioned in the RAF in 1935 and served with No.2 (Army Co-operation) Squadron until 1939 when he became an instructor. He returned to an operational posting in November 1941, succeeding S/L Thompson. He led the Squadron into combat through most of 1942, which included Operation *Jubilee* - the raid on Dieppe - during which he claimed two shared confirmed victories. He left the Squadron soon after that to take command of No.323 Wing, selected to take part of the Operation '*Torch*' in North Africa. On 08.11.42, he took off from Gibraltar in a Hurricane and became the first RAF pilot to land in the new war zone in Algeria. He continued to lead the Wing during the Tunisian campaign, making more claims. In January 1944 he received the command of No.337 Wing in Egypt, which he led to Greece as the Germans withdrew. He flew ground attack missions until the end of the war, and commanded the base at Hassani during the Greek communist uprising. In March 1945 he received an immediate DSO added to the DFC he received in September 1942. He remained in the RAF after the war and served in Malaya against terrorists, retiring from the service in 1957. Pedley is seen here during Spring 1942 when he was leading No. 131 standing or sitting around his regular mount BM420. (*Pedley family via P. Sortehaug - above -*).

Most of the squadron's pilots posing for posterity during May or June 1942. In front of S/L Pedley's aircraft 'Spirit of Kent', most of the pilots are seen posing with some groundcrew. Pedley is holding the Kent White Horse flag with another pilot.
(Pedley family via P. Sortehaug)

The Belgian Flight in No.131 Sqn remains a major step for the Belgians who fought in the RAF, as it formed the nucleus of first Belgian squadron, No.350. Among the pilots who later distinguished themselves in many ways, can be seen F/L Henri Gonay - above - who led the Flight (see biography p9) sitting in his Spitfire named 'Claudine'. At least one other of Gonay's Spitfires, a Mk.V, is known to have been christened 'Claudine' as well.

Left, P/O Désiré 'Guilly' Guillaume, born in 1901, was rather old for a fighter pilot when the war broke out. He had joined the Belgian army in 1918, transferring to the Air Component in 1921 and became a fighter pilot two years later. In 1940 he was a Major, in a non-flying posting, leading the Air Firing School and soon after the French armistice, he decided to flee to the UK. After a brief training, he joined No. 131 at the end of August 1941 but left it soon in October to serve with No.79 Sqn then No.615 Sqn before joining the new-formed No.350 (Belgian) Squadron in January 1942 as B Flight commander. Two months later, he became the first Belgian CO of the Squadron, but relinquished his command in December to take command of RAF Hornchurch. He ended the war as a Group Captain with DFC, and Inspector of the Belgian Air Force in Great Britain. (*via André Bar*)

Henri Picard is another member of the Belgian Flight. Having joined first the Belgian Army in 1936 he eventually joined the Aéronautique Militaire in 1938 but was still completing his training when Belgium was invaded. At the French armistice, he was stationed in French Morocco and instead of returning to Belgium, he decided with many other students to escape to the UK. Completing his training, he was eventually posted to No.131 Sqn in August 1941 and logically to No.350 Sqn in November and in the next few months he claimed three German fighters destroyed, the last being during Operation *Jubilee*. However, Picard was shot down on one week later and became a PoW after having spent six days and nights out at sea until being washed ashore. On 29.03.44, Henri Picard became one of the 50 Allied airmen to be murdered by the Gestapo as he participated in the 'Great Escape'.
(*via André Bar*)

Joseph de Puysseleyr, like Picard, was still under training when the invasion of Belgium took place and, like him, was stationed in French Morocco in June 1940. Reaching Great Britain in August 1940, de Puysseleyr completed his training and joined No. 131 a year later. However, he stayed a few days only to join No.24 Sqn early in December. From that point he became a reconnaissance pilot serving with No.541 Sqn, then No.543 Sqn, and again No.541 Sqn. He was killed on 09.01.45 returning from a mission over Germany while flying Spitfire PR.XI PL900. He had been awarded the DFC in September 1943.
(*via André Bar*)

James 'Orange' O'Meara was the only pilot to received a DSO while serving with the 131. He joined the RAF on a short service commission in April 1938. At the outbreak of war he was serving with No. 64 Squadron and made his first claim, an unconfirmed Ju88, over Dunkirk. In September 1940 he was posted to No.72 Squadron and received a DFC at the same time in recognition of his six victories. He stayed with 72 for a short time before moving to 421 Flight (the future No. 91 Squadron) in October and added a Bar to his DFC in March 1941 for he had now doubled his claims. In October he was sent for a rest. After having served briefly with No. 164 Squadron he started a new tour in January 1943 as a Squadron Leader and took command of No. 131 (County of Kent) Squadron in March leaving it in May 1944 and for his actions was awarded the DSO in the following October. No more operational postings followed after May 1944. He survived the war with about 13 confirmed victories (two shared), one unconfirmed victory, four probables and 12 damaged (one shared).

Above, two British pilots who played a major role with the Squadron 1942, and who later served with No.91 Sqn. Left, John C.S Doll who first served with Nos.258 and 610 Sqns in 1941 before joining No. 131 in November 1941 as a Flight commander. In September 1943 he started a second tour, with No.91 Sqn flying Spitfire Mk.XIIs until May 1944. He ended the war with five confirmed victories - one being shared - and the DFC. On his left, the other Flight commander, Ray Harries. He first served with No.43 Sqn before joining the Squadron in January 1942, remaining with it until December when he was given command of No.91 Sqn. Later he became the Wing leader of the two Spitfire XII squadrons and completed his tour at the end of 1943. In Spring 1944 he became the Wing Commander of No.135 Wing of 2 TAF. He survived the war with 18 confirmed victories - three being shared - with DSO and Bar, and DFC and Bar. (*Pedely family via P. Sortehaug*).
Below, P/O Nathaniel Rowell was less lucky than his two squadron mates, as he was killed on 05.06.42 in combat against German fighters. He is seen here aboard BL327/NX-T 'Rochester' a couple of days previously.

Four pilots who made claims during Operation 'Jubilee' on 19.08.42. Clockwise, P/O Albert 'Al' F. Eckert, an American serving the RCAF, would leave soon to serve in Malta with No.185 Sqn before transferring to the USAAF in April 1943; Sgt John D. Thorogood who was killed in a flying accident in 1946; Hugh S. Jackson and Sgt Horace G. Copland (RNZAF). When the Belgians left the Squadron in November 1941, they were replaced by pilots coming from the Empire and beyond. Like many RAF fighter units formed in 1941, the proportion of non-British pilots was high within the Squadron.

Some South Africans became part of the Squadron, such as 'Bill' Bower from Pretoria (left). He is seen seated in his aircraft with a personal artwork painted under the cockpit, a Springbok to recall where he was from! Bower first joined the SAAF but soon transferred to the RAF in order to be able to fight in Europe. He was posted to No.134 Sqn before arriving at No.131 Sqn in April 1942, and later on served with No.234 Sqn. In May 1944 he commenced a second tour posted to No.33 Sqn then to No.222 Sqn, both units flying Tempests, ending the war as CO of No.33 Sqn. No.131 Sqn became also home of some veterans later in its existence. When Tony Pickering (right) was posted to the Squadron in February 1943 he was commencing his second tour, having served with Nos.32, 501 and 601 Sqns during the Battle of Britain during which he claimed one confirmed victory. He eventually left the Squadron in January 1944. Though the two above mentioned pilots were lucky enough to complete two tours, the fortunes of war were not the same for all, such as 'Taffy' Williams who was killed in a mid-air collision returning from a patrol in November 1942, six months after joined the Squadron. Note the letter 'S' under the cowling, an unusual practice as far as No. 131 Sqn was concerned in 1942.

No.131 Squadron became the operational posting of many pilots in 1941 and 1942, like Arthur Arnot, an Australian from New South Wales. He served for a short time, only three weeks, before being posted to No.1488 Gunnery Flight in mid-July. He was eventually killed in a flying accident on 31.08.42 while flying Lysander Mk.III V9798. Arnot had time, however, to meet John L. Davidson, a Canadian from Ontario who was posted in June 1942, but Arnot didn't live long enough to see 1943 go into action, on 24.10.42.

Not a single Pole served with No. 131, while some Czechs were posted in but for a short time only. On the left, Tomas Kruml, a pre-war Czechoslovakian pilot who had served with the French during the Battle of France. He later escaped to Great Britain and became a founder member of No.312 (Czech) Sqn. He completed his tour with this unit, staying until February 1942. He commenced another tour in October 1942 first with No.66 Sqn, then for a short time with No.131 Sqn, and was then posted to No.122 Sqn until the end of his tour in August 1943. After that he served at various HQ postings. After the war he served with the CzAF and became one of the very few former RAF pilots who were able to serve until retirement without any major problems.

On the right, Otto Smik, one of the very few Slovakian fighter pilot who served with the RAF. He had previously served with Nos.310 and 312 (Czech) Sqns before joining No. 131 in January 1943. He left in March to serve with No.122 Sqn, then No.222 Sqn. In March 1944 he commenced another tour with No.310 and 312 Sqn when he was shot down on 03.10.44. However, he evaded capture and returned to the UK at the end of October. Posted CO of No.127 Sqn in November, his luck left him on the 28th when he was shot down and killed by flak (Spitfire RR227). His tally had risen to ten confirmed victories - two being shared - and he had been awarded the DFC. (*Jiri Rajlich*).

Some French pilots joined the Squadron in 1942 to reinforce the unit. Among them was André Vilboux, who shared the Squadron's first 'kill' with F/L Harries. Still under training when France collapsed in June 1940, he fled to the UK and enlisted in the Free French Air Force in July. Having completed his training, his first operational posting came in December 1941 to 131 Squadron. However, he was posted out in March 1942 to serve with No.611 Sqn, with which he was killed on 19.08.42 after he was shot down in BS179 by Fw190s during Operation 'Jubilee'. He was one of the first Frenchmen to fly the Spitfire Mk.IX at that time.
(*Pedley family via P. Sortehaug*).

Summary of the operational activity
No.131 (County of Kent) Squadron

A/C types	First sortie	Last sortie	Total sorties	Tot Sub-type	Lost Ops	Lost Acc	A/C lost	Claims	V-1	Pilot †	PoWs	Eva.
Spitfire I	07.09.41	16.10.41	20	20	-	3	3	-	-	1	-	-
Spitfire II	02.10.41	26.12.41	73	73	-	4	4	-	-	2	-	-
Spitfire V	20.09.41	19.09.43	1,740	4,396	18	10	28	15.0	-	12	4	-
Spitfire IX	24.09.43	31.03.44	583	583	1	2	3	-	-	2	-	-
Spitfire VII	18.03.44	30.10.44	1,880	1,880	9	1	10	6.0	-	5	-	1
Spitfire VIII	?	?	-	-	-	3	3	-	-	2	-	-
Thunderbolt II	?	?	37	37	-	2	2	-	-	2	-	-
Others												
Magister	-	-	-	-	-	1	1	-	-	2	-	-
Other causes	-	-	-	-	-	-	-	-	-	1	-	-
Compilation	07.09.41	?	6,989		28	26	54	21.0	-	29	4	1

MAIN AWARDS

DSO: 1
DFC: 4
DFM: –

Points of interest :
- One of the very Spitfire units to have used six various makrs.

Unsolved mystery:
Loss of Spitfire MD172

Statistics:
- Lost one aircraft every 249 sorties [Spitfire V I: 244, Spitfire IX: 583, Spitfire VII: 268]
- Nearly half off the combat aircraft losses occurred during non operational flights, a high ratio.

BADGE
In front of an estoile of sixteen points, a horse forescene.

The white horse is the white horse of Kent, the squadron being adopted by the County, and the estoile denotes the sky.

MOTTO
INVICTA

UNCONQUERED

Authority: King George VI, May 1942

Supermarine Spitfire Mk.IA P9433, F/L Henri Gonay (Belgium), Atcham (UK), October 1941.
Taken on charge on 27.03.40, P9433 served with No.92 Sqn then No.610 Sqn and was a veteran of the Battle of Britain. The following year on 11th September, it was issued to the Belgian Flight of No.131 Sqn but served there a short time only, six weeks, before being sent to No.52 OTU on 26 October, and its last flight was recorded on 12th. It ended its career, with the Fleet Air Arm, by October 1944. P9433 was mainly flown by F/L Gonay, especially during the last week of September and the first week of October. It had been christened 'Claudine', a woman's first name of French origin. This Spitfire has received the new Fighter Command camouflage and markings introduced in August 1941 and the serial has been painted on.

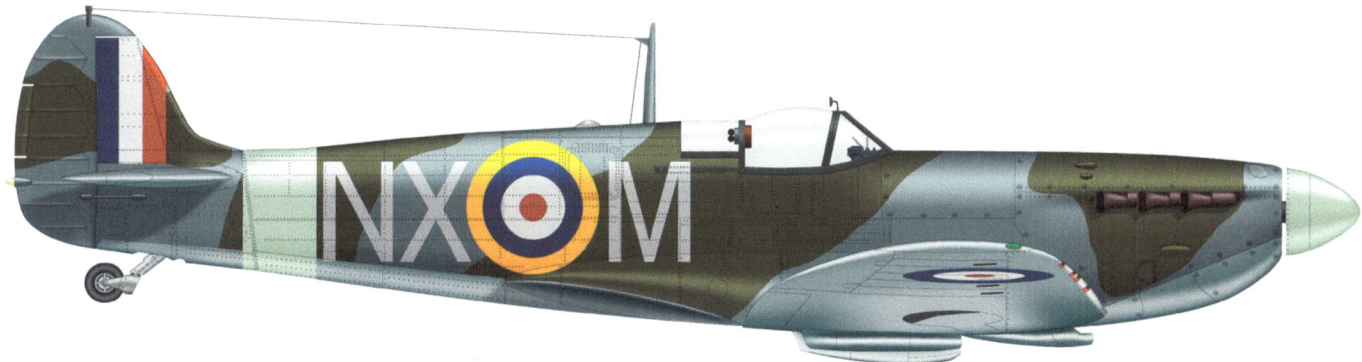

Supermarine Spitfire Mk.IA P9306, Atcham (UK), October 1941.
Another veteran of the Battle of Britain, with No.74 Sqn, P9306 was issued to B Flight of No.131 Sqn in August 1941. It was flown by various Belgian pilots up to 20th October when it was sent to No.52 OTU, then to No.61 OTU, and was damaged in a accident on 04.05.43. It survived the war, however, and it is one of the airframes surviving today. Like P9433 the serial has been painted on following the introduction of the new Fighter Command camouflage.

Supermarine Spitfire Mk.IA X4179, Atcham (UK), October 1941.
Taken on charge on 12.08.40, X4179 didn't spent much time at a Maintenance Unit, being issued to No.266 Sqn three days later. It fought during the Battle of Britain with this unit, but also with Nos.19 and 609 Sqns. By the end of February 1941 it served with No.66 Sqn before being sent to No.57 OTU in March, but was damaged in an accident in May. Repaired, it was issued to No.131 Sqn on 24.08.41 and allocated to B Flight. It was flown by various Belgian pilots in September and October 1941 and, as with P9433, it was sent to No.52 OTU on 26.10.41. It was eventually written off after a flying accident on 24.10.43 while serving with No.57 OTU. Note the underwing roundels painted at the end of the wing.

Supermarine Spitfire Mk.IIA P7746, Atcham (UK), November 1941.
Taken on charge on at No.9 MU on 07.10.40, this was a presentation aircraft named 'City of Bradford'. It served with No.303 (Polish) Sqn, then with Nos.403 (RCAF) and 54 Sqns and again with No.403 Sqn before being sent to No.131 Sqn early in October 1941. It was issued to the Belgian flight and was flown by many Belgian pilots until the Belgians left the Squadron. P7746 continued to serve with the Squadron until crashing on 07.10.41, killing its pilot Sgt H.A. Metcalfe (RAAF). P7746 is seen here having been repainted with the new Fighter Command scheme while serving with 403 Sqn, but the darkness of the tones suggests that it received a kind of mixed grey and dark green for the upper surfaces. Note the serial over-painted but a tiny part of the 'P' is still visible.

Supermarine Spitfire Mk.VB BM420, Squadron Leader Michael G.F. Pedley, Merston (UK), May 1942.
BM420 was taken on RAF charge on 05.04.42 at No.12 MU as presentation aircraft 'Spirit of Kent - Lord Cornwallis'. It was allocated to No.131 Sqn 20 days later to become the personal mount of the CO, S/L Pedley. S/L Pedley used this aircraft through 1942 and made several claims while flying with it. It served with the Squadron until January 1943 and was later on handed over to the Fleet Air Arm for conversion to a Seafire IB, serialled NX923. Its final fate remains obscure. BM420 is seen here painted with the standard Fighter Command camouflage which it received in April 1942 at the factory. After mid-May 1942, the roundels were changed and red paint was added to the older makings resulting in a kind of pink around the older red paint. It is clearly visible on the two photos showing the fuselage and the fin flash. It was probably the first Spitfire of the Squadron to have received the new roundels. Note that the mechanics had not yet altered the underwing roundels.

40

Supermarine Spitfire Mk.VB AD425, Merston (UK), May 1942.
AD425 is another presentation aircraft 'Ardeer Spitfire' taken on RAF charge on 19.10.41. It first served with No.611 Sqn before joining the Squadron on 14.04.41. It served with the Squadron until January 1943, when it was sent to No.306 (Polish) Sqn. It later served with No.316 (Polish), No.312 (Czech) and No.441 (RCAF) Sqns and survived the war. AD425 had its name painted on the port side and it wears the standard camouflage and markings prior to the 15.05.42 when C3 roundels were introduced (even if, when the photo was taken around mid-May 1942, the new roundels had begun to be applied). At that time AD425 was flown by various pilots, mainly NCOs.

BECKENHAM

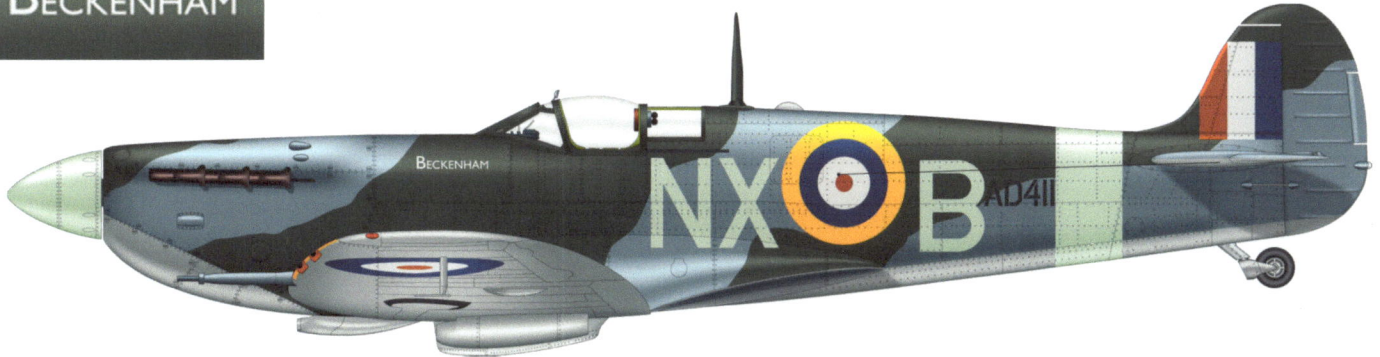

Supermarine Spitfire Mk.VB AD411, P/O Albert 'Al' F. Eckert (USA), Merston (UK), May 1942.
As presentation aircraft 'Beckenham', AD411 was taken on RAF charge on 31.10.41 and was issued to No.131 Sqn on 16.05.42. It was then regularly flown by P/O Eckert from Idaho (USA), but AD411 left the Squadron early in July after a minor accident. It later served with No.412 (RCAF) Sqn and failed to return from a sweep on 28.11.42. AD411 is shown with the standard Fighter Command camouflage and makings in force by mid-1942.

Folkstone + Hythe

Supermarine Spitfire Mk.VB BM632, Sgt John L. Davidson (RCAF), Merston (UK), June 1942.
BM632 had a short career as far as No. 131 is concerned, only two weeks. Taken on RAF charge on 27.04.42 at No.45 MU, BM632 was also a presentation aircraft, named 'Folkstone and Hythe', issued to the Squadron on 07.06.42. It was mainly flown by the Torontian pilot J.L. Davidson (RCAF), and it was in his hands when BM632 was the victim of a burst tyre on take-off on 20.06.42, damaging the Spitfire. Repaired, it was transferred to the Royal Navy and became Seafire IB NX940.

Supermarine Spitfire LF.IX MA834, P/O Stanley A. Catterall, Churchstanton (UK), 4 February 1944.
Taken on charge at No.6 MU, MA834 was first issued to No.129 Sqn on 16.08.43 before being passed on to No.131 Sqn six weeks later. It was damaged in an accident on 04.02.44 on landing (P/O S.A. Catterall) and was sent for repairs, and was then used by No.312 (Czech) Sqn from mid-November 1944 onwards. This aircraft found eventually its way to France after the War. Regarding No. 131, while flying Spitfire Mk.IXs, none were actually assigned to a specific pilot.

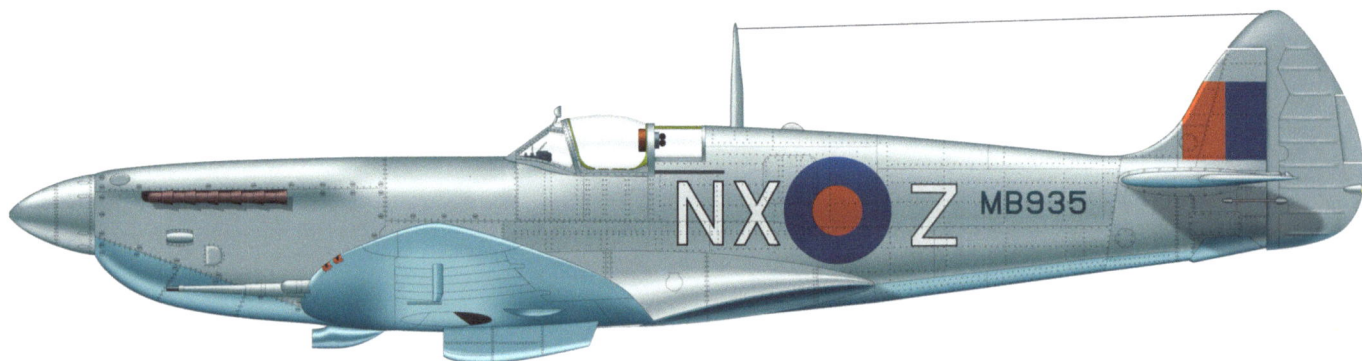

Supermarine Spitfire HF.VII MB935, W/O Douglas F. Philipps (RAAF), Harrowbear (UK), 23 April 1944.
Taken on charge at No.39 MU on 15.02.44, and issued to No.131 Sqn 11 days later. It was flown by various pilots, but it was the Irish-born Australian Douglas Phillips who was in control when the aircraft was lost during a scramble on 23.04.44. Note that MB935 is wearing the standard camouflage for high altitude flight. However, as the photo shows, the code letters were painted with outlined black paint, which seems to have been discontinued later on.

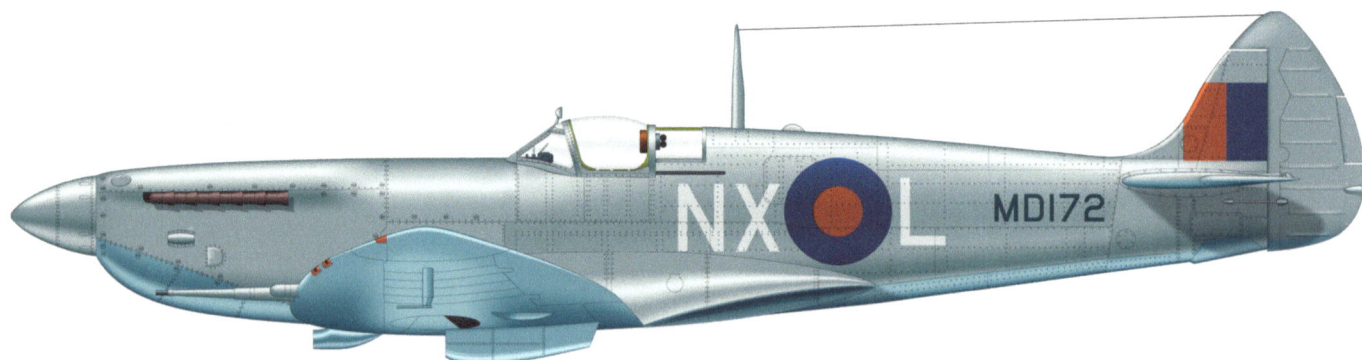

Supermarine Spitfire HF.VII MD172, Culmhead (UK), May 1944.
Taken on charge at No.33 MU on 14.03.44, MD183 was officially issued to No.131 Sqn on 07.04.44. It was used by various pilots during the following weeks. The letters are not outlined, compared with MB983. MD172 was later damaged in operations and after inspection declared beyond economical repair.

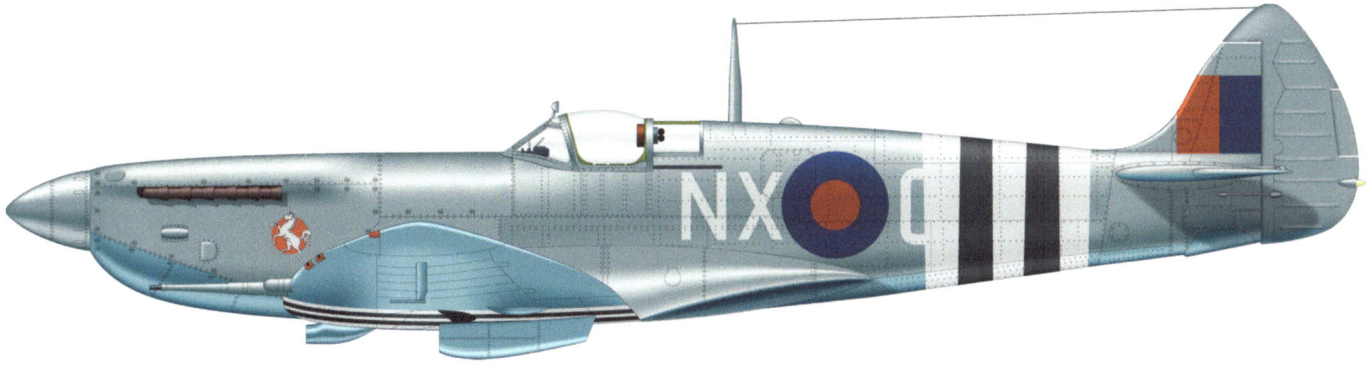

Supermarine Spitfire HF.VII MD120, Culmhead (UK), June 1944.
MD120 was one of the first Mk.VIIs to have been allocated to the Squadron, in February 1944, having been in RAF charge since 24.12.43. Another photo of this air-
craft exists showing the Horse of Kent painted below the engine cowling, so we can imagine that it was still painted there when this photo was taken around D-Day.
Note the D-Day markings have been crudely painted on the fuselage and wings. MD120 continued to serve the Squadron until October and was transferred to No.154
Sqn the following November. It survived the war and was struck off charge in September 1945.

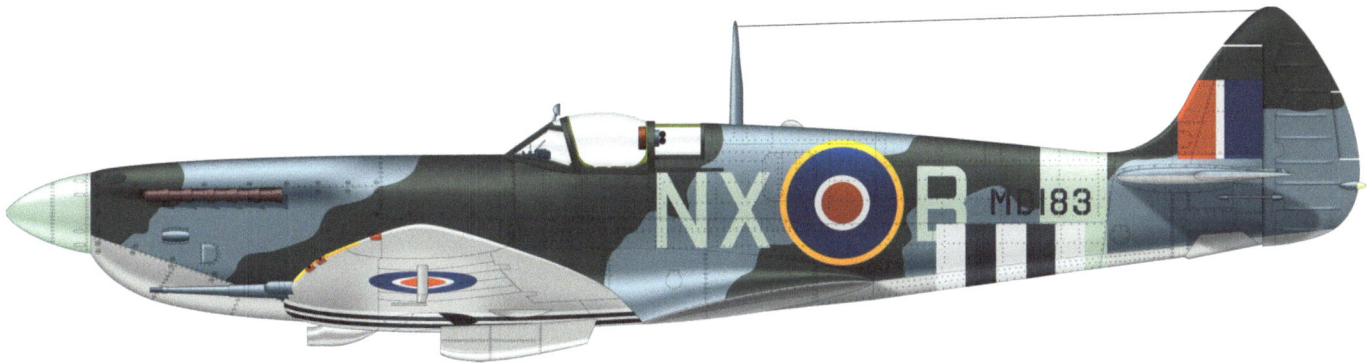

Supermarine Spitfire HF.VII MD183, Culmhead (UK), July 1944.
Taken on charge at No.39 MU on 13.04.44, MD183 was officially issued to No.131 Sqn on 19.06.44 but it appears in the ORB from 15th June onwards. It was flown by
various pilots until the Squadron became non-operational at the end of October. The following month it was passed on to No.154 Sqn, with which it served until the
Squadron switched to the Mustang. It was later used for various high altitude trials and was eventually struck off charge on 09.12.48. It was one of the few Mk.VIIs
used by the Squadron painted with the standard Fighter Command camouflage and markings.

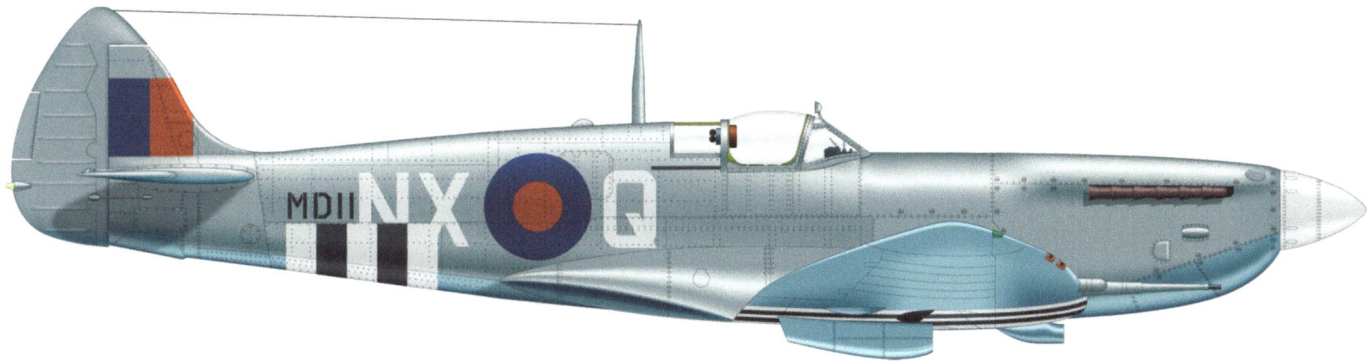

Supermarine Spitfire HF.VII MD111, Culmhead (UK), July 1944.
Taken on charge at No.9 MU on 22.12.43, MD183 was officially issued to No.131 Sqn on 07.02.44 and had a similar career to that of MD183 (see above), being flown
by various pilots until the Squadron became non-operational at the end of October, and then to No.154 Sqn in November with which it served until the Squadron switched to the Mustang. It was later used for various high altitude trials and was eventually struck off charge on 07.12.48. Note the white spinner, an unusual practice
with No.131 Sqn.

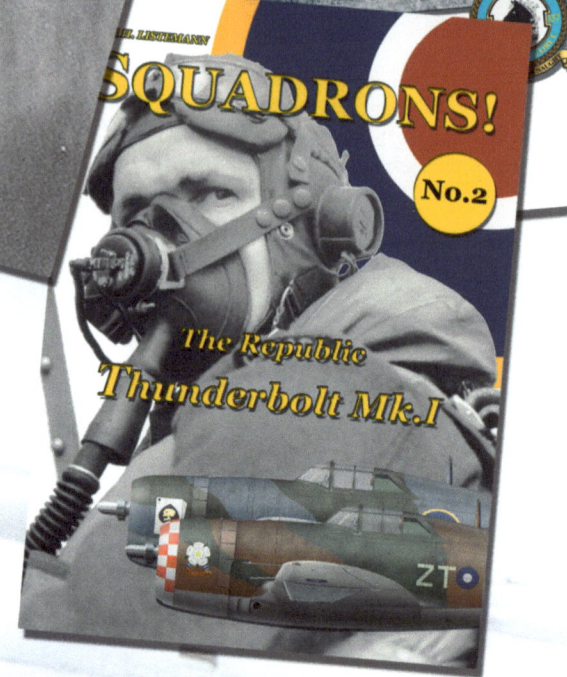

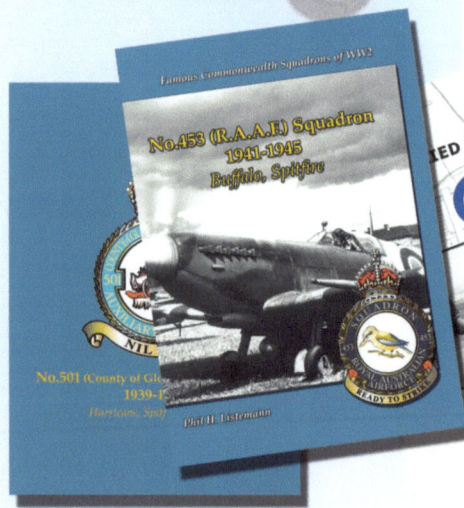

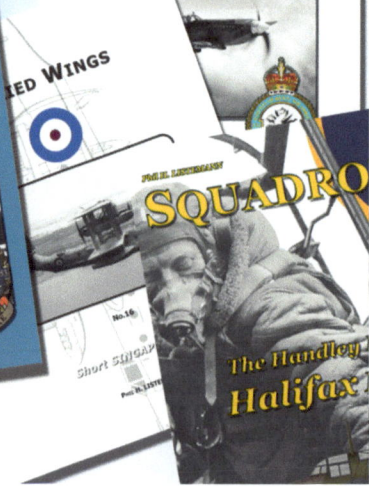

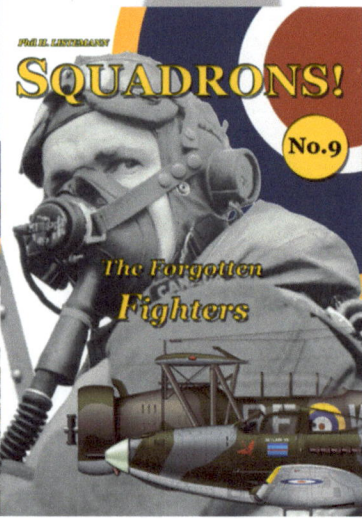

www.ingramcontent.com/pod-product-compliance
Lightning Source LLC
LaVergne TN
LVHW072114070426
835510LV00002B/53